DON'T MISS THE BLESSING

Don't Miss the Blessing

JoAnn Paris Leavell

PELICAN PUBLISHING COMPANY
GRETNA 1990

Library of Congress Cataloging-in-Publication Data
Leavell, Jo Ann Paris.
Don't miss the blessing / by Jo Ann Paris Leavell; foreword by Marge
Caldwell.
p. cm.
ISBN 0-88289-747-0
1. Clergymen's wives—Religious life. 2. Christian life—1960- 3. Leavell,
Jo Ann Paris. I. Title. II. Title: Do not miss the blessing.
BV4395.L43 1990
248.8'435—dc20   89-38308
                                                                  CIP

The King James Version of the Bible has been used for references
throughout this book unless otherwise indicated.

Permission credits

p. 68: From *Giftedness: Discovering Your Areas of Strength*, by Marcia L.
Mitchell. Bethany House Publishers, copyright 1988.

pp. 79-80: John Drakeford, *The Healing Power of the Healing Thought*
(Nashville: Broadman Press, 1981), p. 100. All rights reserved. Used by
permission.

pp. 90-91: From the book *Strike the Original Match*, by Charles R. Swindoll,
copyright 1980 by Charles R. Swindoll, Inc. Published by Multnomah Press,
Portland, Oregon 97266. Used by permission.

p. 152: From *High Call, High Privilege*, by Gail MacDonald. Published by
Tyndale House Publishers, Inc. Copyright 1981. Used by permission.

p. 180: From *Getting Out Of Debt*, by Howard L. Dayton, Jr. Published by
Tyndale House Publishers, Inc. Copyright 1986. Used by permission.

Manufactured in the United States of America
Published by Pelican Publishing Company, Inc.
1101 Monroe Street, Gretna, Louisiana 70053

To Landrum, God's gift to me, who has made being a minister's wife both a privilege and a joy. He is the perfect mate and my best friend.

To my children, Lan, Ann, Roland, and David, who grew up in the fishbowl and are living proof that parsonage life can be fun. *They have always been and continue to be a source of blessing.*

To Lisa, Susanne, and Finis, our more recent additions to the family. Each is a product of God's perfect plan, and became children-in-love as an answer to prayer.

Contents

Part IV: Reaffirmation of the Future

Foreword

The best recommendation for the success of a book is how easily and excitedly it is read! I was with a group of people the other day and we were discussing a best seller. The major comment that came through to me was, "I labored through the first several chapters before I really began to enjoy it."

I have *never* enjoyed a book more from page one than this one! I could not put it down until I had finished it, and I highly recommend it for every woman.

I have known Jo Ann Leavell for many years and have observed her in various roles...pastor's wife, mother, grandmother, teacher, friend, seminar leader, speaker. This is the first time I have observed her as a writer, and she excels here, too. What really comes through "loud and clear" in this book is that her love for Jesus Christ is first in her life—and she is so *real*, so believable. She talks of her failures as well as her successes, and her weaknesses as well as her strengths. She's a positive, warm person, and it shows on every page!

I know this book will be an encouragement to Christian women everywhere, particularly ministers' wives. It will be a real source of strength, a joy, and will provide a great frame of reference no matter what God has called you to do!

MARGE CALDWELL

Acknowledgments

Thanks to Carol Corvin, who typed the bulk of this manuscript and never made me feel any correction was too much trouble. I'm forever indebted for her friendship and skills.

Thanks also to Hellon Freeman, administrative assistant to the president, who has been a constant source of help and encouragement on this project and many others for all the years we've served at New Orleans Seminary.

I am indebted to my husband and oldest son, Landrum II and III, for proofreading the manuscript and offering helpful corrections and suggestions, and to the many student wives who have supported and challenged me to put in print what we have discussed together.

To the First Baptist Churches in Charleston and Gulfport, Mississippi, and Wichita Falls, Texas, I owe an unpayable debt of gratitude for their patience and generosity that made serving them such a blessing.

Finally, thanks to Pelican Publishing Company, owned by my good friends Dr. Milburn and Nancy Calhoun, and to my editor, Nina Kooij, for invaluable suggestions and constant help. I couldn't have done it without all these.

Introduction

I was in Jackson, Mississippi, not long ago attending a stewardship banquet where my husband, Dr. Landrum P. Leavell II, was the featured speaker. Before his message, a businessman stood to give his tithing testimony. He shared his pilgrimage with us concerning his growth in giving. What captivated my attention was his closing statement. He looked out at the large group gathered that night, and said, "Don't miss the blessing."

I don't want to miss *anything*. Those who know me best will attest to that fact. My fear is that many women, and especially ministers' wives, are missing the blessing that God desires for each one of us. How do I know? I have been a minister's wife since 1953, and have been teaching ministers' wives since 1976. Joy is absent in far too many of them. If I have anything to share, it is a positive attitude from a satisfied customer in ministry. And when I talk of ministry in this book, I hope you will see that every Christian woman carries on her own ministry in this world, whether she's married to a pastor or not. Read on, and let me share some highlights from my journey, along with words of wisdom and encouragement for yours.

DON'T MISS THE BLESSING

PART I

Recollections of the Past

CHAPTER 1

LOOK BACK:

Memory Makers

IT IS ALWAYS HELPFUL to take a backward look. When one begins to look back, it is a sure sign of advancing years, and I can tell you now that my hair is gray. However, being a very traditional person, looking back is not hard for me. It's probably easier because of the family into which I married, one steeped in tradition. I married a Leavell. There are lots of Leavells—your paths may have crossed some of them. I'm still meeting family members I have never previously met. My husband's father was one of nine boys, all born and raised in Oxford, Mississippi. Can you imagine Grandmother Leavell—nine boys? Eight of the nine at one time were in religious work. It is a remarkable family.

I had a mother-in-law who interpreted that family for me. She told me all about the family reunions, all about the "brothers," as they called them, and about the sisters-in-law with whom she became close friends. She explained all about that background—people that I now was kin to by marriage, and that was exciting for me.

I recall hearing that Grandmother Leavell became very ill and was slowly growing weaker. Her doctor son, George, came home to Oxford to care for her. George had married, and was ready to leave for China, where he would be the chief doctor in Stout Memorial Hospital in Wuchow.

They hesitated to tell her how soon they would have to leave, but when they did, she smiled, clapped her hands, and thanked God for answering her prayer that one of her boys would be a foreign missionary. George and Frances Leavell left with her blessing and they learned that within the hour they set foot on the soil of China, her beautiful and useful life came to a close. The year was 1913, and yet hearing that story continues to inspire me.

Another wonderful story concerns Dr. Frank Leavell, who was the first Southern Baptist Convention director of the Baptist Student Union. I'm told he turned down the presidency of fifteen colleges to stay at his post and do what he felt to be the Lord's will in his life. Isn't it a comfort to know that money doesn't always talk?!

My own mother-in-law was one of the first women offered a position as educational director. It was in the Freemason Street Baptist Church in Norfolk, Virginia. She also pioneered in Vacation Bible School work, leading the first VBS ever held in a city church in Norfolk in 1921. She was a real "liberated" woman by our standards today, and yet one who still felt her greatest contribution was through her home and family.

I've thought a great deal since about the marvelous contribution this family has made. It has caused me to ask myself, "What am I doing comparable to that?" I'm sure very little, but I think it behooves all of us to think about the legacy we will leave. In fact, John Newport, a cousin by marriage, said in a letter to me following a family reunion, "As in-laws, I think both of us see the great tradition in a perspective which even those who are directly descended do not."

Look at the past, think about the past, and think about your family. What are some of your recollections? I believe the most precious memory you can have is your conversion experience, which sets a spiritual tradition throughout your life. But first, let's look at the importance of family traditions, and how you can build some.

Family Traditions

I heard a seminary professor say that viable, or workable, families are those that prize their traditions. The Leavell family has lots of tradition, and I am so grateful that I had a mother-in-law who recounted the family history for me.

Now, let me remind you that you are the interpreter for your family. Your children will only know things that you tell them about the past. We might call it "making memories."

One of the nicest things I have been asked to do occurred several years ago. I was invited to give a program in my church on Christmas traditions. For abo two weeks before Christmas, I asked everybody I came in contact with about their family Christmas traditions. When I asked what they did at Christmas every year, people would brighten up. I could see that whatever the tradition, it was a significant thing in their family.

I even asked each of my children, "Honey, what is it we do at Christmas that you enjoy? What is it we do every year that means something to you?" I remember one of my daughters-in-law said, "Well, Mom, I love the way that we get together on Christmas Eve. We eat together; we go to the Christmas Eve watch night service together; we come home and open presents together; and we fellowship together." What's the key word? *Together!* It doesn't matter a great deal what we do so long as we do it together.

When I put the question to one of my three sons, he thought about it for a moment and replied, "Well, Mom, we do the same thing, but somehow it's always different." There have been new additions to the family; new children are being born into the family; the kids grow up and are different ages every Christmas. We do the same things, but it's always different.

I asked several teenagers, "What is it you do at your house at Christmastime that has become a tradition?" I never will forget one darling sixteen-year-old, who in her teenage sophistication put her hand on her hip and said, "Well, every year we get in the car and ride around to see the lights." She continued, "We've seen the lights, but every year we have to get back in the car to ride around and see the lights." I smiled, looked at her, and said, "Honey, guess what you are going to be doing when you have kids?" Then she smiled and answered, "Put them in the car, ride around, and see the lights." I replied, "Exactly!" Family traditions are wonderful to look back on.

Before you say, "I didn't grow up in a family like that; I didn't have a family with all of that heritage and tradition," let me say I didn't either! But I looked up the word *tradition* in the dictionary. Do you know what a tradition is? Anything you have done more than once. Do something a second time and it becomes traditional.

The Bible tells us to value traditions. The Scripture says in 1 Thessalonians 1:3 to "remember without ceasing." In Acts 20:31 it says, "watch and remember." The older I get, the more precious my memories become.

I have observed families across the years and wondered why some were closer than others. Why do some spend as much time together as possible, and others never seem to desire that fellowship? There undoubtedly are many reasons, but I believe one of them has to do with the development of these family "rituals." These reinforce family closeness, becoming the glue that holds us together.

According to my readings, these are the positive features of family traditions:

—They make each individual aware of being a part of a common group and heritage.

—They give a certain stability and continuity in a family.

—They impart a sense of we-ness.

—Families with the strongest ties have the most rituals.

—Traditions we build within the family are some of the best gifts we give our children.

—There is something about a family tradition that carries one through when one might be far away, or lonely, or tempted to go astray from family teaching.

—Traditions bind the family together even after the children have established families of their own.

Yet these special moments don't just happen. Because of the hectic pace of our lives, they must be planned—on purpose! I don't think they have to be limited to holidays, but my experience shows that this is a good place to begin.

Here are some Christmas holiday suggestions. Remember, it is the repetition that makes a tradition.

1) Give each child a Christmas ornament every year. If you don't give them ornaments of their own, they may have a naked tree someday! This tradition will provide them with memories as they trim their own tree in later years.

2) Serve a birthday cake for Jesus. Children especially will remember this. I heard a unique variation of this tradition not long ago. The mother makes a three-layer cake. The bottom layer is

chocolate, representing the blackness of sin. The next one is red, indicating the blood of Jesus shed for that sin, and the top layer is green for the new life in Christ. She ices the entire cake in white, symbolizing the purity of the Christian life. As it is served, she has a marvelous opportunity to explain the plan of salvation to the younger members of the family and any friends who might be present. Good thinking, huh?

3) Read the Christmas story. We always let the youngest child read, and my children say you haven't lived until you have suffered through the Luke passage with David!

4) Go caroling—out or in. Music has a special appeal at Christmastime. We never had a piano player but are thrilled now to have a daughter-in-law, Lisa, who can play!

5) There are those who use their Christmas cards as a prayer list for the new year. A new twist would be to write a note of encouragement to the ones for whom you've prayed.

6) Repeat menus for Christmas eve and Christmas day. One or two dishes may be optional, but some "every year" family favorites must be included. We have good friends who have a tradition of Mexican food on Christmas Eve. What about you?

7) How about a family shopping trip? One of our department stores had a section provided for kids only, with no item costing more than three dollars. I remember well letting our children shop there for family gifts, learning early how to make decisions.

8) Every year I decorate my house *early* in December so I can enjoy it as long as possible. My son says there is not a spot that doesn't jingle or glitter! I have never been able to enlist a lot of help from the male members of our family, but I have to believe they enjoy the fruit of my labor.

9) Do you have a ritual for the opening of gifts? We do. When the big moment arrives, we sit around the tree and pass out presents, one at a time. This prolongs those happy moments as long as possible.

10) What about closing your celebration by sharing some spiritual goal for the New Year? I can't think of a better time.

Don't be discouraged if everything you try doesn't work. We still laugh about the year I planned a worship time of Scripture, music, and prayer. I even had a written script for everybody. The only problem was the first one to participate got so tickled he could not even read! We finished amid the chuckles, but I'm not sure how much true worship was experienced. All traditions will not have spiritual significance, but it is a wonderful teaching tool when they do.

Thanksgiving lends itself well to tradition. We never fail to go around our table sharing blessings for which we are grateful. What about place cards with a personal affirming message for each member of the family or guests? Including those who have no close family can be another nice Thanksgiving tradition.

We developed a tradition of our own the eleven years we were in Wichita Falls, Texas. There were two other families with no nearby relatives, so we got together and worked out our own plan. Josh Moore fixed a country ham and biscuit breakfast for all of us *every* Thanksgiving morning, and then we alternated Thanksgiving dinner between the George Ritchies and the Leavells. Our children still remember the front-lawn ball games that followed those eating extravaganzas. This was a tradition mothered by necessity, but one that blessed our family.

We are *big* on birthdays at our house. We emphasize them with favorite family dinners, gift giving, and that little extra attention we all enjoy. I had a friend whose first grandchild was expected close to the date of his own birthday. Thinking it would please him should the events coincide, I suggested that possibility. I'll never forget his response. He didn't want it born on his birthday. He didn't want to share that day. That was *his* birthday, and he did not want the attention divided.

My mother-in-law was one who tucked notes inside lunch boxes, notebooks, briefcases, or suitcases for out-of-town trips. We never left her home without finding a note inside the lunch she always packed us for the trip. What a great way just to say, "I love you."

Start traditions simply. Begin holding hands for the blessing (a *wonderful* tradition), and yes, in restaurants, too. It is an opportunity to witness in this pagan world of ours, and it is the soothing predictability of traditions that make kids feel secure. Children love things which happen again and again, the little things that give a family feeling, like hearing their parents pray.

Our oldest grandchild could say Psalm 100 when he was three

years old. Why? Because it has long been a tradition in the Leavell family to repeat that psalm anytime we travel. I know that is not considered the travelers' psalm, but it is "our" trip psalm!

How about going out for breakfast on the opening day of school? Adults need traditions, too. I had a friend who had a coffee the first day of school every year to celebrate "no kids!"

Try getting yourself a red plate that says, "You are special!" Use it for any cause for celebration or recognition. A celebrating family is a happy family! Let's make these precious moments count. We can establish roots that will be nurtured, pruned, adapted, and passed on to future generations.

What a legacy of memories we can leave our children and grand-children! Make a child happy today, and you will make him or her happy twenty years from now by the memory of it. This will give your children a head start on life.

Spiritual Traditions

Besides these family traditions, the main thing I want you to look back upon is your salvation experience—that moment in time when you invited Jesus Christ into your heart and life. Can you remember back that far? Perhaps for some of you it hasn't been that long. For me it was in 1941 (and for any who may be wondering, I was born in 1931). I was ten years old at the time I invited Christ into my heart.

I remember it so well because we had just moved from Atlanta to New Orleans. My dad was transferred with the Federal Reserve Bank to manage the branch in New Orleans. I was the last of five children and grew up almost like an only child—one of those change-of-life babies who came along late. I well remember the Sunday my mother and daddy went forward to move their church member-ship. I was left on that pew all by myself. I can still remember the loneliness I felt even though there were a large number of people in the church that day, and I realized for the first time that my parents had something that I didn't. I think the Lord used that experience in my life, because it was only a few weeks until I asked Christ into my heart.

I wanted to state my decision publicly in our church, but my mother wouldn't let me. She thought I was too young to know what

I was doing. However, I must have been convincing because I got her consent. I can go back to that experience regardless of what happens, and that's my anchor. That's the stability to which I hold every day I live.

Someone said you can stand any "what" if you've got a "why." The "why" for you and the "why" for me is our faith in Christ. I don't know which "whats" are going to come in your life. You will encounter some I'll never meet.

You may confront economic difficulties. We have seen a whole bunch of that in some regions, haven't we? Many people have been laid off from jobs due to a faltering economy in their area. Maybe the "what" in your life will be a sick child or that you can't have children. The "what" in your life may be one of any number of things, but you can stand with a faith in Jesus Christ. If you don't look back to that experience frequently, you'll lose your motivation for following Him. We must remember what He's done for us in the past, so we can realize what He can do for us in the future.

Our pastor once preached on a passage that I didn't really know was there—Revelation 3:3. This is what it says: "Remember therefore how thou hast received." Have you done that lately? Have you recalled the moment of your salvation? That's the "why" for all the "whats" that may come into your life and into mine. (Please see Appendix B, on "What It Means to Be a Christian.")

When our oldest son, Lan, was in high school, he played on a winning football team. I don't know how good he was, but because of their record, he had numerous college scholarship offers. I can remember giving him my best mother lecture. "Honey, you've got to know you are where the Lord wants you. You can't be swayed by all of these nice things that they're saying to you, but you have to pick the college where you know the Lord wants you." I painted the darkest picture I could paint: "When you get to Mississippi College in the middle of August and it's hot, when nobody else is on campus but football players, you're having two-a-days and you're dying. Plus being hundreds of miles from home, you have got to know that you're where the Lord wants you."

Now I believe that. I convinced him of it, and, sure enough, when he was going through two-a-days, when it was ninety-plus degrees in August, and he was 600 miles away from home, he had the assurance he was where he should be. That kept him going. That's the "why," that knowledge, that commitment that we make to Christ—whether it's in salvation or a daily experience we have with Him. Lan could always go back to that assurance when it got tough.

I tell the ministers' wives in their class at the New Orleans Baptist Theological Seminary (where my husband is now president), "When you know you are in the church the Lord wants you to serve, regardless of how ugly deacons act, or how 'tacky' the Woman's Missionary Union ladies treat you, regardless of all these things, you will have that personal support system." You will have the "why" for any "what" that comes into your life. Your salvation experience provides a spiritual tradition that you can go back to again and again.

Look back! As you do, you will feel the significance of your family traditions, and build them for your children. And you can relive your most important memory and draw strength from it—the memory of your conversion. Most of us realize that conversion is not completion, so we move from that remembering experience to our daily walk.

CHAPTER 2

LOOK BACK:
To Childhood

LET ME ASK YOU SOMETHING. If we understand that the

Father loves us, and the
Son died for us, and
if we are assured that the
Holy Spirit lives in us,

then why is it that we have trouble seeing ourselves as people of worth? That's a mind-boggling question.

I'm told that seven out of ten of us don't see ourselves as having value, and that adolescents have the lowest self-image of any age. "Low self-esteem" are the words we use today. Years ago we called it "inferiority complex." But nothing has changed. It's those same feelings about ourselves.

If we are average humans, and I'm assuming we are, that means 70 percent of us have such feelings. That's not hard for me to believe, because I have had them. I have suffered from a low self-esteem. That's one of the reasons for my interest in this subject. When I make that statement in classes at the seminary, students say, "Mrs. Leavell, surely you don't have an inferiority complex, you don't have a low self-esteem." Oh, but I do. The one thing I've learned is how to hide it! We all know there are things we can do to cover it up, but that doesn't make it go away. I can fool the world, but at 2:00 A.M. it's just *me.*

I did not realize how widespread this problem was until I began to share something of my insecurity. The feedback I got was over-whelming. Why are we so fearful of taking off our masks? We put on our "everything is perfect" faces and scare our friends off with our pretenses of perfection. We protect our reputations and often forfeit our chances to minister.

The thing that encouraged me to share my real feelings was a statement I read that said, "People cannot relate to a person who appears to have no problems." The most encouraging thing we can do for others may be to *admit* we have need. From time to time people tell me, "You look like you always feel good. You don't look like you have a problem in the world." Actually, I'm a past-fifty wife, mother, and grandmother with all the trauma that comes with the turf.

Low self-esteem often affects our marriages, because when we suffer, we make others suffer also. Our experiences in childhood are carried over into marriage. My husband could tell you of the struggles we have had because of my low self-image.

Landrum has good self-esteem. I can't tell you exactly why I am not so blessed, but I'm not. My insecurity is there, and it's very real.

What is self-image anyway? It is one's conception of one's self or one's role. It is the picture in your mind of who you are—plus or minus. It is not based on truth, but what you believe is true. Most of these pictures were developed in our past—our childhood.

I have had scores of ministers' wives in my seminary classes tell me of their struggles with low self-esteem. Many were talented, able individuals with no reason whatsoever to feel insecure. Remember—it is *not* based on truth. I have known others from disadvan-taged backgrounds with little education who were extremely confi-dent. It's really a paradox. However, I've read, "A weakness under-stood can be a strength." Let's try to understand a little about this problem.

As I look back, I can recall some experiences which may have contributed. I never remember my mother or daddy telling me they loved me. You may think that's crazy. Call it what you will, but it is true. They provided well. I grew up not wanting for anything. I was the last of five children, so by the time they got to me they were comfortably fixed. I had anything in this world I wanted, and I'm grateful, but I still never remember feeling unconditional love. It is trite but true that only in a world of love can we unfold and bloom.

A prevalent attitude is, "I show my children that I love them." You've got to *tell* them, too. I didn't hear those words for twenty-one years, so Landrum can't tell me enough now. I am so glad the Lord put me with him since my family did not express affection. In fact, when we were dating, he asked me one time, "Honey, do you ever kiss your daddy?" He still laughs at my answer: "Well, yes, if I'm going on a trip!" You see, the Leavells are hugging and kissing folks. When I married into this family, I didn't know how to handle it, but now I love it! I absolutely love it.

They say that a child's life is like a blank piece of paper. Every person who walks through this life puts a mark on the paper. Think about it. There were many people who put marks on my paper and yours. You're putting marks on the paper of your children's lives right now, and we need to understand how self-image is formed in the background of children. We can help give them a good solid background now. That's why I love the title of a book by Anne Ortlund, *Children Are Wet Cement*. We have the ability to mold them and make them and put prints on them before the cement hardens. Mine is hardened, but children are still pliable.

I also heard a story about an elephant, and I can believe it is true. When an elephant is small, when it's newly born and weak, the keeper puts a little chain around one leg and attaches it to a stake driven in the ground. The elephant tries to move and cannot because of the chain. The elephant grows and becomes a giant, and guess what? He still doesn't move from that tiny little chain, because he simply doesn't know he can.

Most of us are chained from childhood and don't know we can free ourselves from sinful limitations. Our minds are programmed from these early experiences. We don't know the Lord can free us through faith in Him as He leads us on a day-to-day basis. What about your childhood? You tell me what sort of childhood you had, and I can tell you what you're likely to be. That's a spooky thought, but I believe it's true.

Look for a moment at some of the causes of low self-esteem. Comparing yourself to others and programming self-doubt are factors in this problem. But first we'll examine the role played by negative influences. Certain personal traits may be the product of a negative environment. Such an environment can shape a child's life, its effects continuing on into adulthood.

Negative Influences

Consider all the influences that surround us daily. The media is a good example. What percentage of the news on TV or in the newspaper is positive and wholesome? And think of the traffic patterns of your life. How many really positive people do you encounter in a day's time? Few, if any, I imagine, and negativism is every bit as contagious as a virus. Negative thinking saps our strength and makes us *weak*.

I heed the advice, "Don't traffic with a pessimist." Stay away from pessimists if they have an adverse effect on your spirit. I look for people who cultivate a positive outlook.

Often you find people in the Lord's work who are marked by this critical, negative spirit. I recall being at supper with one of these not long ago. After several attempts to turn the conversation to a more positive bent, I finally realized I was getting nowhere. It is a chore for me to be around those afflicted by this mind-set. They seem to have no joy and certainly give no joy.'

Are you like that? A checkup at this point may be in order. Listen to your conversation and determine if you are part of the problem or cure for the negativism in our society.

How do you answer the simple question, "How are you?" The majority of people who ask that are not interested in a medical report. It has been said that a neurotic is a person who when asked, "How are you," tells the whole story! Most people who hear your troubles don't care anyway, and some are even glad you're having them! How much better just to answer, *"Super,"* and it could be we will act our way into a new way of feeling.

I've heard it takes eleven positive inputs to overcome one negative one. This means when you tell your child one time, "You're bad," it's necessary to tell him or her eleven positive things to overcome that one.

My daughter told me once—and this hits home—"Mama, you're not quick to tell us things we do right as much as things we do wrong." I'm guilty! So for her birthday I went to our pharmacist, who thought I was crazy when I declared, "I want a bottle of empty capsules. I want you to put this name on the front and type on there, 'Take one a day for fourteen days.'" I brought those capsules home, where I had written down fourteen positive things about my daughter. I rolled up the little pieces of paper and put them in the capsules. I gave her other things for her birthday, but in her letter to me she said, "Mama, my favorite present was the little bottle of capsules." She continued, "I didn't know you thought all those things." Somehow, I had failed to communicate those positive characteristics to her.

I wonder how many of us leave things unsaid. Our married children need affirmation and encouragement; our single children need it; our mates need it. We live in a negative society so we've got to make up at home for those things they're going to encounter out in the world.

Mary Crowley, founder of Home Interiors in Dallas, used an illustration which helped me. She said if you put a drop of ink in a pitcher of water, it clouds the water naturally. Do you know how many pitchers full of clear water it takes to bring back the clarity in that one pitcher? Thirteen! Isn't that amazing? That one negative word we speak, that one put-down we plant in the mind of a child or mate, will take an awful lot of making up to overcome.

In my background, "well done" was never heard. If I made a B+, why wasn't it an A? If I made a C+, why wasn't it a B? My dad especially was never satisfied. I think at some point we need to accept the things that our children do, especially if they're making an honest effort.

Maybe you can recall when your mate demeaned you with a verbal cut or your parents criticized you. Think back to teachers who put you down. My son-in-law got his doctorate in 1988 at the seminary. We are proud of him, but we are even more proud because a high school guidance counselor told him he would never make it through college. Isn't it a good thing he didn't accept that? It's great that somebody else along the way told him he could achieve.

Negative communication tears us down, but positive communication builds us up. I can recall those in my past who built me up.

I remember a teacher in high school who called me in one day and said, "Jo Ann, we have a student body election coming up." She named a girl she hoped would win that election. She went on, "I'm told you could be of great help in campaigning for her and helping her be elected." What did she say to me? That I had the ability to help her, and she thought enough of my ability that she wanted to use me in that election. I will never forget Mrs. Yancey, because she made me believe I was somebody. We *all* have that ability to communicate positively.

Verbal put-downs are among the most subtle forms of child abuse. You would not be guilty of child abuse physically. We are indignant when we read of such, but destructive criticism does fall into the category of psychological abuse. We need to be careful what we say to children, because labels like "stupid," "lazy," or "troublemaker" often become self-fulfilling prophecies.

I remember using a few of those adjectives on our daughter, Ann, when she was in grade school. She had such a strong will and resistance to anything Landrum and I suggested that we almost despaired of her completing her education. One day I was describing some of her antics to friends, and said in Landrum's presence, "We don't have to bother putting any money away for her college education. She'll be in the penitentiary by the time she is fifteen!" He looked at me with that look any wife would recognize and said, "I don't *ever* want to hear you say that again. You are going to give her a reputation she has to live up to."

We poison one another on a day-to-day basis with our critical words. Did you know that verbal poisoning is a leading killer of marriages? If you have a low self-image from childhood, you bring it into marriage, then if it's fed by a negative mate—you can predict the results.

Poor self-esteem grows when it's fed. Therein lies the tragic story in a nutshell. Marriage should be the institution which enhances the "becoming process." We seek to become all Christ wants us to become. When we come into marriage, it's a responsibility of mates to lift us up and help us. I'd hate to think what would have happened when I brought my low self-esteem from childhood into marriage if Landrum Leavell had not supported me. Suppose he had continued to belittle me, to tell me of all my failures and faults? I'm here to tell you I don't think I would have survived. I would have been destroyed somewhere along the way. But he has encouraged me, helped me, and has done what I needed in this becoming process. He has encouraged me to become what I am and hopefully what the Lord wants me to be. This is what marriage is all about. However, we bring the baggage from our backgrounds—all the negativism and ridicule that has touched our lives from so many different sources.

Our discouragement over past mistakes contributes to our feelings of insecurity. Have you ever failed? Of course you have. I've heard that failure is a normal accompaniment to a busy life. If you seek to do anything, in some areas you are not going to succeed. In his book, *Falling into Greatness,* Lloyd Ogilvie states, "If we never fail, we miss the reliability of His gracious arms." Celebrate failure! You learn more through mistakes than any other way.

Landrum may not remember this, but I recall when our oldest son ran for an election in high school, and lost. He came home, and I thought one of the neatest things his daddy ever said to him was, "Son, do you know when I won my first election? After I came to the seminary. I never was elected to anything in high school." He didn't put him down for failing. He didn't ridicule him for losing the election. What did he say to him? It's all right not to win. You're not a bad person because you lost. So often we tell children, "You're worthless, you did this. . . ." There is a big difference in being a bad person and doing a bad thing, or making a mistake in an active life. We must be careful not to let past failures or someone else's evaluation rob us of our self-esteem. Let's help our families. Let's build up one another.

We Must Not Compare!

The futile desire to compare with others is another factor contributing to a bad self-image. You see, all of us are both learned and ignorant, just in different ways. I remember when we enlisted a teacher in the adult division in our church at Wichita Falls. He had a doctorate in science, but he was scared to death to take this class. I remember Landrum telling him, "Listen, you don't need to worry about those in your class. They are probably illiterate when it comes to the Bible." I think we often assume because someone has a doctorate, he or she also knows everything there is to know about the Bible, or vice versa. Not so! We have different areas of expertise.

It is unfair and unprofitable to compare areas of personal weakness with someone else's strength. Why? Because when we do, we always come up short—always!

It's intimidating to feel everyone else knows how to do things right. I'm good at that. I look at people and think—well, I can't do what she does, or I can't do what he does. Therefore I conclude I'm not worthy, or maybe useless. Not so! No one else in the world can be you or me, and we are far from bankrupt. We have unique skills, we have differing gifts. We have divergent aptitudes and experiences.

I have had experiences you have not had. I have survived four teenagers! If I don't have any other claim to fame, I would like a sign that says, "I survived it!" They have turned out to be good kids. I had my own abilities, and I have particular skills for my calling.

There are things each of us can do and we must focus on what we can do, not what we can't do. Make a list of the areas in which you know yourself to be competent: I *am* a good cook, I *can* organize effectively, I *do* my job well. We can change our self-image by developing a more positive attitude and refusing to berate ourselves continually. Otherwise we may set standards of perfection that are unrealistic.

I have one friend who says that when she makes her agenda for the day, she always does so as though she had two people helping her. Aren't we good at that? We set abnormally high expectations for ourselves. When we don't measure up, we have a sense of failure. If we are candid, we will realize that some people have more energy than others. I've always been blessed with energy, but I have friends who are not so blessed. That is not to my credit, the Lord just made me that way. I tell my class of ministers' wives, "You may not have the energy, the physical makeup, the last preacher's wife had." We need to be realistic about what we can and can't do, then follow the Lord instead of the expectations of our peers or our church members. Our confidence cannot be wrapped up in someone else's package.

I thought one of the most perceptive things Landrum said after we moved to Wichita Falls was when he went to get his shoes shined. There was a black man named Roosevelt who shined shoes in the barbershop. When Landrum walked in, Roosevelt said, "Oh, you are the new preacher at the First Baptist Church." Landrum replied, "Yes, I am." Roosevelt then stated, "You are the one who has come to take Dr. Landes' place." Dr. Landes had been there eighteen years. Landrum said, "Oh, no, you've got that wrong. I didn't come to take Dr. Landes' place, I came to make a place for myself."

Why is it we think we have to take somebody else's place? We are uniquely gifted. It has taken me all these years to figure that out. God has made me a special way for a special purpose.

I am usually an energetic person, but when I was pregnant with my second child, I had zero energy. Those first three months I felt I could not get out of a chair. I got better and felt wonderful, but I can remember telling my best friend how I felt those early months. I said, "I feel draggy; I don't have any energy." She's always had a low energy level, but for me it was a new situation, and I had become impatient with myself as I compared it to my earlier energy. We must not compare!

The Tape of Self-Doubt

Another matter we must avoid is the tendency to program self-doubt and criticism. "This is something I have never done, I can't do this, I can't do that." We play that mental tape over and over and over again. Do you know what the Scripture says? "As a man thinketh in his heart . . ." What? "So is he." That's like that chain around the elephant's foot. He doesn't know he can move. If he keeps telling himself he can't move, he can't. If we keep playing those tapes and programming ourselves, we will never do all the Lord intended us to do.

What you and I need to learn is that we can reverse the tape. I have spent a lifetime trying to switch channels from negative to positive. I have spent a lifetime trying to teach my children and to give them a good self-image and assure them I love them. I tell them every chance I get. We never hang up the telephone without saying, "I love you."

Surely you understand that those words come easier to some people than others. I know. I have seen it in my family. It is harder for me to speak them, for instance, than it is for Landrum. And again, I didn't grow up with the phrase. Perhaps that's part of my difficulty now, but I believe there is something in my nature which makes it hard. Our four children have grown up with us saying, "I love you, I love you, I love you," and it is still easier for some of them than others. It's not all background and childhood experiences. It's just something about the way we are that makes it difficult. If your mate or your children have trouble expressing affection, be patient.

My mother never said, "I love you." After I became convinced that this was not the way to live, I made the effort to become closer to her. I knew I needed to do something, so I began writing it—I was chicken! I wrote letters to my mother and signed them, "I love you." You see, by an act of will I could do that. She would write back—"Love, Mother." I would write again, "I love you." She'd write back, "Love, Mother." This went on for years. Finally, I graduated to the point that I could say it on the telephone, and when we'd hang up I'd say, "Love you, bye."

I *did* live long enough for her to tell me verbally *once.* It was such an effort, and she wrote it on rare occasions. Tell your kids—whether they answer or not, tell them. Tell your mate whether he answers or not, "I love you, even if you can't love me back." This is one of the healing things that we need to do. A letter like the one below will make it all worthwhile. It came to me during the writing of this chapter from our middle son, and I will never believe it was anything but providential. Please take note of the "29 years." I hope it will encourage you to continue planting—the harvest *will* come.

> Dear Mom & Dad,
>
> At Ray Benton's funeral yesterday I had the opportunity to reflect on parents and their role in the development of their children. Ray had six children and all were in attendance.
>
> It seems that parents have a thankless job. When they are doing the most for their children, the children appreciate it the least. By the time the children get old enough to recognize the price the parents have paid to educate and raise them, they are too busy with their own problems and families to express appreciation or are too proud to make this admission. For 29 years that has been the case with me.
>
> With the two of you slowly approaching the age of Ray, I wanted you to know that I agree with the way you raised me and appreciate the sacrifices that you made to raise 4 kids. I can't think of anyone else with 4 kids that doesn't have at least one outlaw or one child

that won't speak to them. That is a true testimony to both of you and each day the Lord allows the two of you to remain with us is a blessing.

I feel the two of you have upheld the honor and spiritual standards which the older generation of Leavells exemplified. In the words of Steve Green, "May all who come behind us find us faithful."

Thank you for your love.

ROLAND

The expression of positive thoughts like these can help reverse the tape of self-doubt so many of us hear in our heads. Say the words "I love you" as often as you feel them, and seek out those who will tell you too!

Forgive the Past

I'm sure you've taken some side trips since this chapter began, thinking of your own background. I don't know where you are or where you are coming from. Maybe those prints on your paper are not what you would like them to have been. Just remember, you can't unscramble eggs! Leave the past behind. As I discussed in the previous chapter, the past can provide some wonderful sustaining memories, but don't dwell on the bad points. Everything that you have experienced is, purely and simply, *over!* Don't waste energy on what might have been.

Give up the fantasy of having some of the significant people in your life change. Accept the fact that your "irregular person" may never change or give you the love, acceptance, and approval you desire. Hurt is a part of life. We are all going to be let down, even rejected at times.

Tucked away in every life are wounds and scars. We are *all* "handicapped." You can see mine, I cannot see yours, but these handicaps do hinder us. The problem is not within you, but within them. You can never make up for what your parents or others failed to receive in their childhood. Perhaps there were conflicts and family experiences that made them the way they were which they never took time to work out. Look for approval and love from those who have the capability of giving love. Someone stated, "Emotional maturity means recognizing and accepting what has happened in your life without seeking to place blame or regretting your past." Let go of the sad yesterdays—anticipate the tomorrows.

I believe at some point you have to forgive the past. Maybe it was an alcoholic father. Maybe it was a mother who was not a stay-at-home mother and you felt neglected when she wasn't there in the afternoon to greet you when you came in. Maybe it's a teacher who put you down, or that mother-in-law you can't abide. Maybe it's a sister to whom you were compared all your life, and you have this "thing" about that sister. Maybe it was a brother with whom you had difficulty. I don't know who or what it is, but at some point you've got to be willing to forgive. Don't be content to be a helpless product of your environment. You simply *must* make peace with the past, and whatever it was that caused you to be in the seven out of ten with low self-esteem. Remember that *no one* had a perfect childhood!

There is an ancient saying which states, "There is no saint without a past, and no sinner without a future." We have got to break our childhood bondage. Forgiving turns off the tapes.

The successful man or woman is the one who carries the best qualities of childhood into adulthood. Turn loose all that was not desirable, and bring the best qualities of the past into your present marriage and your later years.

We must deal with the past before we can move on. Have you dealt with it? Perhaps one of the most healing passages in the Bible is Philippians 3:13: "Forgetting those things which are behind, and reaching forth unto those things which are before." Don't let yesterday usurp today.

Have a time of acceptance, if necessary. Ask the Lord to impress upon you the fact that you are loved, accepted, and forgiven. Claim His love by faith, and ask Him to free your mind. If there are still things which trouble you, ask Him to continue stirring up your mind. Carl Sandburg said, "Life is like an onion. You take off one layer at a time, and sometimes you cry." We must take off every layer of hurt, giving it to our Heavenly Father in prayer.

I read that hurts are like abscesses. They are raw. They cover over with a scab, then something comes along and knocks the scab off, and it hasn't healed under there. Only the Lord can truly heal from the inside. We need to open the wounds for healing to begin, but don't continue opening and reopening old wounds. Settle the matter once and for all, and move on.

Forgive! Forgive yourself and forgive those significant people in your past. Wounds heal only through forgiveness in order for healthy growth to begin.

Let's pause right now. Think about your life. Whatever those hurts are, let them go. Experience the miracle of inner healing. Begin by praying this prayer of sincerity.

Our Father, Thou art the heart-knower. Thou dost know the heart of every person on this earth. Thou dost know every event that has made up our lives as we live them today. Teach us, Lord, the ways of forgiveness. May we never forget that Jesus said, "As we forgive our debtors . . ." May we not come to Thee asking for Thy forgiveness for sins without willingness to forgive the sins of others. This very day, help us to take a long step toward a healthy self-esteem, a clearing out of all the underbrush of the past, allowing the spotlight of Thy love to reveal every dark place. Forgive those dark places and restore to us, we pray, full spiritual health and vitality. Bless our homes. May they enjoy the relationships of two spiritually healthy people every day and in every way, in Jesus' name. Amen.

PART II

Recognition of Internal Support

CHAPTER 3

LOOK WITHIN:
Practice the Presence of God

BEING ASSURED THE PAST has been covered by the grace of God, we need to take positive steps to correct some of the difficulties our low self-esteem has created. This is therapeutic and good for renewal of courage. In this book I am going to suggest three ways to cure this age-old problem.

1) Practice the presence of God (Chapter 3).
2) Promote others (Chapter 4).
3) Paint the house (Chapter 5).

I will explore the first point here, and explain the others in the following chapters.

I taught in a Sunday School department for many years with a man who had a Ph.D. degree in chemistry and who taught at a local university. His favorite statement was, "I believe you ought to practice the presence of God." When I hear that phrase, those days come back to me. It was a life-style with him to practice God's presence.

It should be a life-style with all Christians because Christ is the source of all our healing. If we reject Him, we reject wholeness. If we are trying to move in the direction of wholeness this is the place to begin. Every time Jesus appears in the New Testament, He is trying to meet needs. He will meet our needs today if we let Him.

The past can offer us wonderful things, such as the family traditions I discussed earlier. Yet it can also hamper us with deep-rooted insecurities. Overcoming our past—eliminating low self-esteem and the feelings of inferiority that many of us have built up since childhood—has to be a cooperative effort between us and the Lord. We need to be reminded constantly that we are God's work of art. Isaiah said we are called, created, and formed by Him (43:7). He also said God would never forget us (49:15). God made us and abides with us. He created then, and He recreates now.

Have you invited Jesus Christ into your heart and life? You may say this is a funny question to be addressing in a book for Christian women and ministers' wives, but stranger things have happened. Can you look back and *know* beyond a shadow of a doubt that you are saved—a born-again Christian? You may not know the exact day and hour, but you know this transformation has come about in your life.

I have never forgotten an example I heard a Sunday School teacher use a long time ago. She drew a line on the blackboard indicating the road of life. She said we somehow believe we are going to come to a fork in the road, take the correct path, and live happily ever after! Then she reminded us we are *never* promised a fork. Repentance means you are going down this road of life, then realize you are a sinner and can't go it alone. You invite Christ to come into your heart and take control. It is *not* a fork. It is not "someday I'll think about God." Repentance is a deliberate, conscious, voluntary turning from the habits, practices, and activities of the old life. It is an inward change which manifests itself in an outward change. You go back in the opposite direction toward Him. You see, the "far country" is anywhere you have chosen to live apart from God and His influence on your life.

We need not be bad to be lost. As I described in the first chapter, I was saved when I was ten years old, and I don't think I had ever done anything terribly wrong. I knew I was a sinner; I came to that moment of need. I never will forget, if I live to be a hundred, the blessed relief I felt when I confessed Christ. Wholeness comes to those who make a faith response.

This is trust in a person, the person of Jesus Christ, by a voluntary act of will. No two conversions are exactly alike. Just as we are unique, our salvation experience will be tailor-made for us. Gail MacDonald reminds us that we cannot be turned on for Jesus until we have been turned on by Him. We can't stir up the fire unless it has begun at some point in time. Don't waste your time trying to stir up your adult class or your class of young people in Sunday School until they have been turned on by the Lord.

He Loves Us

John 3:16 declares, "For God so loved the world, that He gave His only begotten Son, that whosoever believeth in Him, should not perish but have everlasting life." He loved us so much that He gave His only begotten Son. Our love is in response to His love Who first loved us (1 John 4:19).

If we have accepted Him at any point in life, He saved us, and promised us His presence. He affirms this over and over again in the Scripture: *we are loved.* When you begin to grasp the extent to which He went to prove His love, you can practice His presence on a daily basis.

Good self-esteem grows out of being loved or feeling we are loved. If we did not experience love as a child, this is an important part of the rebuilding process. How do I know I am loved? I can read numerous Scriptures which declare this. My husband tells me, but even if I didn't have him, I have the Lord Who does. When I recognize that reality in my mind, I can overcome the problem of low self-esteem. We must understand our value and importance to Him, and begin to treat ourselves with the same regard God has for us. We can begin to blossom in the light of God's unconditional love.

Apply Jesus in the area of your past. Ephesians 4:23-24 admonishes us to "be renewed in the spirit of your mind," which simply means to change your thinking. We can only do this with the Lord's help. We must let new thoughts soak into our minds to counter all those unpleasant messages from the past. Do you grasp what I am saying? We are reversing those tapes, and just as in any learning process, repetition is important. Repeat to yourself, "I like myself unconditionally because I am a child of God." "I will not devalue myself with self-criticism." "I can do all things through Christ Who strengthens me." With practice you can program your mind to think positive thoughts. Don't despair if you fail to control your thoughts completely. It takes *time* to bring about lasting change. However, when we discern old thought patterns surfacing, we can stop them. Refuse to dwell on them.

One of the surest ways to accomplish this change in our thought patterns is by practicing His presence. Make it a practice to feel precious to God. The devil is the one who wants to destroy us (John 10:10). Jesus came that we might have abundant life—not just life, but the *abundant life*. "I am the good shepherd, and know my sheep, and am known of Mine" (John 10:14). This is the relationship that's ours. "I give unto them eternal life, and they shall never perish, neither shall any man pluck them out of My hand" (John 10:28). Fellowship may be broken, but not the relationship. We have heard those verses over and over again, but have we really understood their message? When you are unsure of your worth, remind yourself of these promises from our Heavenly Father.

Feed your mind on high thoughts of Him, and practice His presence. When your faith begins to grow, wholeness will come and blessings will follow. Accept God's evaluation, not the evaluation of others or even your own. Someone said, "You wouldn't have to worry about what people think of you if you only knew how little they did!"

The first step in curing a low self-image is practicing the presence of the Lord. This is not a kit, but must become a way of life. You are going to be shot down along the way. Feelings of insecurity will return on occasion, but move them aside and continue your chosen course of action. It would have been nice for me to have my parents' approval, but I have God's approval and my own. What I do from this point on is *my* responsibility.

He Knows Us

God even knows our names. Don't you appreciate it when people address you personally? Make it a practice to call people by name. Our middle son, Roland, came home from the church preschool one day when he was small, and said, "Momma, Mrs. McGinnis calls me Ronald." I responded, "Tell her your name is Roland." He said, "I do, Momma, and she still calls me Ronald!" We like to be known by our names.

Our pastor said his mother would always remind him of three things when he left home for any reason:

1) give people a firm handshake
2) look them in the eye
3) and say your name with confidence.

The Lord told Moses, "I know you by name." If we practice the love of God and the presence of God, we can know who we are because of *whose* we are. This is that unimaginable love He has for us, undeserved yet real. Carry that thought with you through the day, every day.

The Lord spoke to Jeremiah, "Before I fashioned you in the womb I knew you; and before you were born I dedicated you; and I designated you a prophet to the nations" (1:5). Not only does He know us, He made us, and He called us to do a certain job.

I heard a testimony recently by a friend of mine recalling a camp meeting experience. One of the ladies in the church looked her in the eye and said, "God has something special He wants you to do that no one else can do." That statement penetrated my friend's heart, and she surrendered her life to the Lord, though unsure of where or how she would be used. At this writing, Esther Burroughs is in charge of women's evangelism with the Home Mission Board.

That is part of this package of practicing the presence of God. We must know we are loved, and that He made us, knows our names, and has a place for us. When we program that into our minds, we are moving toward a better self-image.

Imaging is another suggestion for developing a healthy self-confidence. This is simply picturing the Lord with you. You may think that is juvenile, but don't knock it if it works! Whatever can help you develop in the area of self-esteem is beneficial. Picture the Lord with you; imagine His Holy Spirit in you at all times. Do you think about Him when you go to the grocery store? You are taking the Holy Spirit with you. When you go to church, the Holy Spirit goes with you. He is in you, and anywhere you go, He goes.

I can remember years ago Landrum preached a sermon to young people on some of the social evils. He reminded them if they went into bars they were taking the Holy Spirit with them. That sermon made an impression on me. We need to be reminded that if we go in undesirable places, His Holy Spirit goes with us if we are Christians.

Imaging can work another way also. If you find yourself in frightening experiences, picture Him with you. If you are speaking in public for the first time, imagine He is there. Remember His presence when you teach a Sunday School class. When you go to a new pastorate and are scared to death, just know the Lord is with you. He is not only in you, but even ahead of you, leading the way.

Psalm 139 affirms there is *no place* we can get away from the Lord:

> O Lord, Thou hast searched me, and known me. Thou knowest my downsitting and mine uprising, Thou understandest my thought afar off. Thou compassest my path and my lying down, and art acquainted with all my ways. For there is not a word in my tongue, but, lo, O Lord, Thou knowest it altogether. Search me, O God, and know my heart: try me, and know my thoughts: And see if there be any wicked in me and lead me in the way everlasting.

Read Psalm 139—it is exciting. I don't care where we go or what we do, we cannot get away from Him if we are His children. I don't want to get away from Him. I want Him to be with me every step of the way.

Growing in Faith

The Christian life is the development of a Christlike personality, growing up spiritually. This maturing process takes time and involves struggle. There are no shortcuts. If there were any, I would have found them, but any transformation in our lives is gradual and progressive.

If there is no opposition to our growth, it means one of two things. It either means that we are not Christian, or we are not giving the devil any competition. If you don't meet the devil head on every morning, it may mean you are going the same way he is. If we are living for the Lord, we are going to run into Satan constantly because He is not going to like what we are doing. He can't own us but he can mess up our testimony. If there is no opposition to your spiritual growth, you probably are not doing anything.

I don't know about you, but I want some direction in my life. I want some growth to be evident. Can you see that you are closer to the Lord than you once were? In fact, if there was a time in your life when you were closer to the Lord than you are right now, you are a backslider. He hasn't moved—you are the one who has moved. If you are like I am, growth has been sporadic at best. It will take determination and *some* struggle to straighten that out.

This decision to grow is something no one can force upon you. It must be your choice. In a sense I despise the word *choice* because it puts the monkey on me. I can't decide for you nor you for me. I have talked to mothers who would love to grow up for their children, but this is up to the kids. It must be their choice. I hope for the sake of your marriage, as well as your work, that you will choose to begin this process of spiritual growth. You must understand the importance of "seeking first the kingdom of God and His righteousness. Then all of these things will be added to you." It must begin here.

I want to tell you what I have seen in living color. In the pastorate I was involved in weekly Bible studies with women. I could see them growing. They were involved in reading and studying the Bible, growing by leaps and bounds. Where were their husbands? Yes—at work. She was growing, he was working. Now that we are out of the pastorate and at the seminary, where are the husbands and wives? The men are growing and the women are working—exactly the opposite of before. When one spouse is not growing, a dangerous imbalance results. It is a threat to any marriage.

I'm aware most of you reading this book are out making the living. Fifty percent of ministers' wives are in the work force. The others are taking care of the kids and carrying numerous responsibilities. Your time is limited, but you *must* involve yourself in some learning and growing experiences. This is the best thing you can do, not only for yourself but for your marriage. I hope you understand that. You choose whether or not you grow. You must make a conscious choice *not* to let stagnation happen. When you are not involved in any class or formal learning experience, it takes real commitment to do it on your own. What is commitment? The best definition I've read is, "the ability to carry out the task long after the mood has passed that caused you to make it." This is something you do because it is right to do. Meet God every day whether you like it or not. This is your gift to Him.

Gail MacDonald reminds us in *High Call, High Privilege*:

> Ministry is far too draining to be sustained without the experience of the inner fire. Women cannot survive in the fishbowl if they don't stay close to the fire.

That is such good advice. And don't think for a moment our priorities are something we straighten out once and for all. No way. This is something we straighten out *every* day, *every* week, and *every* month of our lives.

Mrs. Dawson Trotman, the widow of the founder of the Navigators, said, "A wife's most significant contribution to her marriage is her steadfast walk with the Lord." I have also heard, "A woman filled with the love of the Lord is the most beautiful wife a pastor could have." This is the greatest thing you can do for your husband. *His* spirituality is not enough for you. Secondhand faith is not sufficient; faith must be an individual commitment.

There *are* going to be times when you fail. The hardest thing to maintain is your quiet time. When those times come, just pick yourself up, take yourself in hand, and get back with it. It is not a sin to stray—it is a sin to stay there.

Four spiritual disciplines can help us to practice the presence of God in our lives, and grow in our faith. These are: regular worship, silence, daily Bible reading, and prayer. Let's take an in-depth look at each one.

Regular Worship

What can we do to prevent stagnation? As they say, "The journey of a thousand miles begins with the first step." Let's begin our spiritual disciplines with regular worship. It is essential—and we must continue it even if we don't feel like it. We live in a "feel like it" society, and that is never to be confused with Christian commitment. You are not going to have a high-mountaintop experience every time you go to church. That's unrealistic. It is just like regular eating habits—some meals are more exciting than others, but the important thing is we are fed.

I think of how many there are in our churches suffering spiritual malnutrition. They are too immature to feed themselves, and neglect the opportunities for others to help them grow. Jesus admonished us not to forsake "the assembling of ourselves together, as the manner of some is" (Hebrews 10:25). I might add Jesus practiced what He preached. "As His custom was, He went into the Synagogue on the Sabbath day . . ." (Luke 4:16).

What sort of things might keep you from church? Maybe you are glad when your kids are sick and you have an excuse not to go. Do the same things that keep you from worship on Sunday keep you from work on Monday? Check your spiritual temperature.

I can remember some less than exciting worship services the Lord blessed. One in particular stands out in my memory. We had a college choir visiting to perform a concert of sacred music on a Sunday night. I was bored stiff, did not enjoy their choice of music, and was much relieved when the program came to an end. Landrum stood to give the invitation, which he always did. I remember thinking to myself, "What a colossal waste of time since nobody could have possibly been moved to decision by such a dry, dull service." Before those thoughts were completely formed in my mind, I looked across the aisle as my own son, Lan, made his way to the front, surrendering his life to the ministry. You see, the Lord doesn't need my permission to work, and He can bless lives in mysterious ways when His people gather for worship.

In God's plan we are to have three homes: a family home, a church home, and a heavenly home. Our church home provides the nurturing ground for our faith as we are surrounded by those who love us and assist us in growth. Seek out those places and people where Jesus really is, where His Holy Spirit is moving among God's gathered people.

Have you chosen the best church available for your needs and those of your family? You see, churches have personalities just like people. The challenge is that after three years a church will take on the personality of the pastor—and his wife! What sort of atmosphere are you providing?

We had the opportunity to be in the Soviet Union recently. Along with three other couples we were there to work in the churches. What we experienced among those faithful Christians will forever be a part of our lives. They put us to shame with their faith, forged in extreme persecution.

Revival is being experienced there. Baptists are extremely small in number but those faithful Christians are praying the revival going on in their church will spark spiritual awakening in the Russian Orthodox Church, the only group with the power structure to reach that land. *Then* they stated, "If that happens, it will have to take place *over* the ministers or priests." How sad.

Some may think we in the ministry get instant spiritual benefits from handling religious things in our jobs. Let's remember that doesn't necessarily add to our spiritual growth as individuals. We must maintain our regular worship in church just as carefully as we suggest to others, if not more so.

Landrum always said that among his most sobering thoughts was the realization that his people were not going to grow any closer to the Lord than he was. We cannot lead others where we have not been. The growth of our membership is at stake here, plus, what about our children? They will be the first to sense whether our habits are born of conviction or are job oriented. Kids are smart and won't be fooled by a fake.

The thing that sold me the textbook I have been using for my seminary class was a caption on the front cover which read, "Tending the inner fire so others can share the warmth." Isn't that what it's all about?

I have always felt at home with the people of God. As a child, I can remember looking forward to fellowship with my church family. In fact, I can probably attribute my love for the church today to those who provided such a warm encouraging atmosphere as I was growing up. It's been said that "God has called us from our relationship to the world, and summoned us to His family." He connects us to the rest of God's people like parts to a body.

We forget sometimes the church is "family" to many people. I guess that is why I hate to hear of churches calling off services, especially during holidays. For scores of widows, singles, and children with disinterested parents, the church and its fellowship form the center of their lives. Who knows, the time may come for you and me when all we will have is God and His church. Don't neglect it. An old saying is applicable here: "The time to fix the roof is when the sun is shining." Regular worship, in good times as well as bad, practices the presence of God and nurtures the growth of our faith in Him.

Silence

Next, let's consider silence before God. A little quiet time every day to recharge our batteries is essential—time to think, meditate, and listen to our Heavenly Father. The Scripture says, "Be still and know that I am God." I'm not sure about you, but being still does not come naturally for me. I'm not sure it comes naturally for anybody. The Twenty-third Psalm says, "He leadeth me beside still waters." If we desire tranquility, it will only come when we pause in our frantic pace to let Him lead us. He is going to speak to us in direct proportion to our willingness to be silent before Him.

"Tarry" was Jesus' instruction to the disciples before the coming of the Holy Spirit, and could very well be His instruction for us today. This is when He is going to impress His will upon our hearts. In those rare moments, haven't you had the Lord lay somebody on your heart whom you needed to call, write, pray for, or witness to?

I have a friend who calls me every now and then. She will call and say, "I just had a feeling I ought to call you." You can't believe what a good feeling that gives me. Why? Because I know she is open to the Lord's leadership. Have you ever had those feelings? If you have, chances are it happened when you were silent before Him. I have another friend who says, "Don't move until God gives you a promise, or you will accept second best." Try it. Cut off your motor and be still and know God. "Many a restless woman just needs to climb up on God's lap and sit awhile," was Mary Crowley's advice.

We live in a world where some people feel they can get along without God. They are convinced they can accomplish almost anything by their own ability and determination. I don't know *anything* I need more than to slow down, pause in my busy schedule, and listen for His voice. There is therapy in that. We need to practice silence.

One of the things I learned from a book on stress is the part noise plays in our stressful lives. I had never thought about it before. We live in a *big*, noisy world. If you stop to listen, there are noises all around you. In a subtle way that grates on us, and increases our stress level. We need to block out those noises of our overinvolved, busy lives, and listen for the still, small voice of God.

I never will forget a story I heard once. There were men working in a place with sawdust on the floor. One of them lost his watch. They looked and looked but were unable to find it. They decided to break for lunch before looking any further. A little boy who overheard the conversation found the watch and returned it to the owner. When asked how he found it he replied, "Well, I just put my ears to the ground, listened, and went where the tick was!" In a sense this is what we do when we are silent before God. We listen, and then move in the direction He indicates.

I know what you are thinking. "I have three kids. When in the world am I going to find any quiet?" I'll be the first to tell you it is not easy. My house is a zoo. If the phone is not ringing, the doorbell is. All I can tell you is, it is worth the effort. I don't know what time will work best for you. This will change with your circumstances— with the ages of your children and with other variables in your life— but quiet time is valuable and worth working for.

I fight the same battles you do with distractions. Our untrained minds rove over the many things we have to do, and the deadlines we face. We must constantly call our minds back to God, redirecting our thoughts to our goal of uninterrupted communion with Him.

I've heard this called "Holy Inactivity." One problem with our culture is that we equate success with being busy and overscheduled. We often attribute inactivity to time wasted, and we feel we are too busy to "waste time."

If you equate the presence of the Holy Spirit only with activity, there is going to come a time when you can't be physically active. I saw my mother, who was a busy person, reach this period of forced inactivity. When that happened, she felt completely useless and lacked joy.

I determined right then to try and develop an intimacy with God that would see me through bad times as well as good. Karen Mains said at a conference I attended:

> In crisis, are you still looking to God to prove Himself or do you *know Him so well* you believe He is working in your behalf? Many people go through life without that quality of recognition. At least

one evidence of spiritual maturity is the time it takes to get to God in trouble.

That sort of intimacy, just as in marriage, must be cultivated.

I read the testimony of a man who admitted 90 percent of his quiet time was spent in asking God for things and 10 percent in gratitude and petition. When he began to practice silence with care, these statistics reversed. He now spends 90 percent of his quiet time on listening for God's will and 10 percent on requests.

"Whatsoever ye ask in My name I will do" (Mark 11:24). With power like that available, we need to be sure what we ask is in keeping with His will.

Praise God during your silence. Praise is a healer—not just in time of panic, but on a regular basis. Read Scriptures that refer to Him. Bask in His love and express gratitude for His goodness. Are you grateful to God for His blessings? One benefit from remembering your salvation experience is to cause gratitude to well up within you. Most of the feasts in the Bible were simply experiences where the participants could thank God and look back to His providence in their lives. Think about the Lord's Supper. That is its purpose. We look back to His broken body and His shed blood and we feel grateful.

I love anybody with a thankful heart. Teaching your children gratitude is a parent's responsibility. Do you remind them to express thanks? If praise is on the lips, it stems from gratitude in the heart. If you are not grateful, chances are you are not going to praise. I read, "If you can think of nothing for which to give thanks, you have a poor memory!" Praise Him for Who He is and anything He has done for you. Thank Him for every good thing in your life. It will truly surprise you what the Lord has done!

Not only are we to thank God, but one another. Anybody who has been in my seminary class knows my emphasis on thank-you notes. This will be dealt with in detail in chapter 11. But remember to use your silent time with God wisely—your spirit will be so rewarded!

Daily Bible Reading

The third thing I would suggest to bring about spiritual growth is daily Bible reading, at least one chapter. Someone has said, "God will not reveal what is not written until we do what is written." I'm told we remember 10 percent of what we hear for twenty-four hours. That percentage jumps to 15 to 30 percent when we read. If we study, which implies the use of a pencil, we remember 60 percent. This is why I encourage my students to underline, star, or circle as they read. This increases retention and, of course, the ultimate retention requires memorization. Commit Scripture to memory and it will always be with you.

I got "turned on" to Bible study about twenty years ago with a fill-in-the-blank sort of study on the Christian home. As I looked up Scriptures, traced words in the concordance, and made daily application to my needs and those of my family, I began to grow. That is why I am so hung up on the value of preparation for church and seminary classes. I'm convinced that if a Christian does not seriously study the Word of God, little learning is going to take place.

I began that study with a friend. We agreed to meet at my home every Monday afternoon at 1:30. I found the value of being accountable to someone. I knew she was depending on me to be ready to discuss any problem areas at that time. It was wonderful discipline, and ended up being perhaps the greatest turning point in my spiritual pilgrimage so far.

Another helpful study my daughter, Ann, and I did for about a year was Partnership Bible Study in Craig Massey's *The War Within You*. This study appears in my first appendix here, and I urge you to try it. It had the same element of responsibility to another that brought about faithfulness on my part.

A workbook, *Don't Miss the Blessing Study Guide,* accompanies this material for that reason. Only as we think through and apply our study will it have a significant effect on our lives and ministry.

There are many ways to study the Bible. You might begin with books, personalities, or themes. I learned a great deal doing a study of the women of the Bible. From these women we can learn valuable lessons. I'll never forget how I profited from my study of Abigail, Hannah, Sarah, and Mary who was chosen to be the mother of our Savior. Each of these women possessed qualities worthy of emulation.

We must examine everything in the revealing light of God's Word. It is our main avenue of knowing what is right, and God is not ever going to lead us contrary to His Word. If we listen to His Word, He will teach us His will.

We had a deacon in one of our former churches living an immoral life. When questioned about it, he said, "We believe this is God's will." Of course that affair wasn't the Lord's will. He will *never* lead you or me contrary to His written Word. Mark that down!

Ruth Graham, wife of Billy Graham, suggests keeping your Bible open somewhere in the house. Do you have a desk, chair, or definite place for your time alone with the Lord? Most of us need the discipline of a time and place. Keep some devotional books, and a notebook or what some refer to as a spiritual journal so you can take notes as the Lord teaches you. I wish I had begun this practice years ago, but it is never too late.

Prayer

Cultivating a sense of the presence of God also comes as a result of genuine prayer, when we feed our soul on high thoughts of Him. Bible study and prayer go together like wings on an airplane. If we only have one, chances are we will just go around in circles, but with both we will move ahead in our spiritual pilgrimage. Prayer is a time when we get close to Him, ask His help for our daily needs, and just have joy in His presence. Someone said, "Whoever practices this will soon excel in virtue."

These are those moments with the Master that keep our spiritual batteries charged. Don't neglect Him. "Always maintain the habit of prayer" is good advice from Colossians 4:2.

It takes real desire and discipline to put aside all the activities that normally claim our attention to pray. We have to believe daily prayer is important. No matter how busy we are or how many children we have, we must *make* the time.

I remember vividly when Landrum and I first moved to New Orleans from Gulfport, and our son Roland was a student at St. Martin's High School, across town. He had a ride in the morning, but I had to pick him up every afternoon. Any way you cut it, the trip took an hour out of my afternoon. With numerous responsibilities, I found myself resenting this, what I considered to be "wasted" time.

I began to pray about my attitude and several thoughts surfaced. When else would I have thirty uninterrupted minutes with my sixteen-year-old? If I prayed all the way to school and talked to Roland all the way home, was my time really wasted? I don't think so.

The psalmist said, "My soul thirsts for God, for the living God" (Psalm 42:2). Do you have that sort of desire to be with the Lord? You may have to begin praying for that desire, since people rarely drink until they are thirsty. Tell God that you are willing to be open to all He wants you to do.

In the spiritual realm, a time with the Lord each day produces growth in the Christian life. Just as surely as meat and potatoes going into your system become muscle, skin, and bone, so a prayerful study of the Word of God becomes spiritual food and flows through you to produce the fruit of the Spirit—love, joy, peace, etc. (Galatians 5:22). This power will flow in direct proportion to the vitality of our deepening relationship with Him, and perhaps we will be able to say with Brother Lawrence, "I suddenly found myself changed."

Landrum and I have a friend who always uses his commuter time for prayer. In a conversation with Landrum, he described what he felt to be development in his prayer life. He said, "Before I get halfway to work now I am through with my gimme's!" Can you see any progress in your spiritual walk? A good exercise may be to evaluate your present devotional life. Make a commitment to regular worship, silence before God, daily Bible reading, and prayer. If you don't do those now, *begin*. We can never move beyond the priority of practicing the presence of God. His presence and love brings us security in our lives.

A pastor's wife planning for missionary service asked, "What do I take to the mission field?" Three things were suggested by a longtime career missionary:

1) The right attitude.
2) *A deep commitment to time with the Lord.*
3) A good close relationship with your husband.

I would say "ditto" for *all* Christian women, especially ministers' wives. Otherwise you will *miss the blessing*.

CHAPTER 4

LOOK WITHIN:
Promote Others

AFTER PRACTICING THE PRESENCE of God, a second thing I would suggest
in building self-image is to promote others. This follows in natural
sequence because it is only as we know we are loved that we will know
how to love others. When we realize the depth of Jesus' love, then
we can experience true wholeness by sharing with others.

A proven way to help yourself is by helping other people, because
when you seek happiness for others, you find it yourself. That may
sound simplistic, but it works. The Scripture says in Proverbs 11:25,
". . . he that watereth shall be watered also himself." Have you ever
done something for somebody else—whether it was to write a note,
take a gift, or give a compliment—that didn't make you feel better?
It has a *wonderful* psychological effect. This concern will, in part,
help you overcome the low self-image that many of us possess.

If 70 percent of us need to improve our self-image, then we
should try to help others build theirs up. Break the cycle of thinking
about yourself and your problems, and think of others. Someone
said, "By the simple device of doing an outward, unselfish act, you
can make the past recede. The present and the future will again take
on their true challenge and perspective."

The saying, "There is no greater invitation to love than in loving
first," is certainly true. I didn't know how to love for years until I was
loved. I began to notice what made me feel good and if it made me
feel good, then it was logical it might make somebody else feel good.
Do some things for people you have experienced and enjoyed. Love

unused or generosity kept to oneself is wasted. If we merely receive from the Lord and receive from other people, that is selfish, isn't it? The cardinal sin of most of us is our reluctance to share our faith, our failure to "pass it on." We sit around getting our "cups full," and enjoying each other to a fault. The end result of a full cup should be the overflow. If you have received, then be generous and contribute to the well-being of others. It will help them as well as build your own self-image. You see, no one is useless in this world who lightens the burden of another.

There are a couple of things you can concentrate on that will help promote others. One is to affirm the importance of those around you, and another is to use your own spiritual gifts to serve others. In this chapter we'll take a look at these.

Be an Affirmer

A decision to become involved with others requires a choice. We can continue to play tapes of the past or we can move into the world as affirmers. Go out and affirm other people, minister to others, and move everyone you can toward Jesus.

Who are the affirmers? They are those who communicate their admiration of us, who verbalize their love. I looked up the definition of *affirm* and this is what it means: "To validate, to confirm, to state positively, to uphold." Anytime we are involved in such actions we are in the affirming process. Who are the people in your life who have done this for you? I want you to think about them, and if they are still living write them a note of appreciation. It is never too late.

This need for affirmation is no new problem. Go back and think of the verses in your Bible that have to do with encouraging one another—the New Testament is full of these passages. Hebrews 10:24 says, "Let us consider one another . . ." Hebrews 10:25 calls for "exhorting one another," and that simply means to encourage. Hebrews 13:13 says that we are to "do it daily." Daily we are to be involved in this affirming or encouraging process.

Charles Swindoll calls discouragement the devil's calling card. Satan would love to get us discouraged and keep us discouraged. However, we can be used by Him to encourage. There are many lonely people in this world, and loneliness is the ultimate poverty.

They feel isolated, unloved, and are without self-esteem. We can be used in loving them and helping them to feel needed.

We can be used in church to dissolve cliques. This is one of the cardinal sins of most Baptists. We get self-satisfied in our little circle of acquaintances. I confess my guilt at this point.

I remember specifically that when we moved from Gulfport, I didn't want to go. We had been there seven years and I *liked* it. I am one of those who puts roots down *deep*. I liked my neighbors, my friends, my church, and where I lived. I'm not one of those who is ready to move every eighteen months. I want to plant my life. When we were deliberating the decision to move, I wasn't open to it at all. Landrum told me, "I don't know anyone who *needs* to move worse than you do." When I asked him why, he answered, "You have your own friends, your little routine, you don't need anybody else. You need to be jolted, shaken up and forced to make some new friends." That was harsh, but he was right.

When we moved to New Orleans, my little routine was shaken up *good*. I began to understand how the stranger feels. Landrum was traveling much of the time when we first came to the seminary. My youngest son was still at home, and he and I would go to church supper and prayer meeting alone. Following supper, David would get up and go to graded choir. There I was. I didn't know anybody. There was a little group at this table, a little group at that table, and another little group over there. No one seemed to care that I wasn't included in any of the groups.

I am aggressive enough to make friends. However, a lot of people are not like that. I have talked to student wives who did not leave their apartments for six weeks after coming to New Orleans! They were completely intimidated by the big city. They needed a friend. Don't wait for the Lord to shake up your routine. Shake it up yourself and begin to minister to these lonely, discouraged people who lack self-esteem and need a friend. The Lord can use us, and the need is there.

John 13:35 says we are to "love one another." Romans 13:8 says we are to love one another and to love our neighbors as ourselves. You can't love your neighbor as yourself if you don't love yourself. I am not talking about conceit. There is a big difference between conceit and self-esteem. One is within you and one is because of the Lord. You need to love yourself in the best sense of that word. Believe that you were created in God's image, believe He has gifted you, because if you don't believe that, you will not be very useful in His kingdom. When you begin to understand that you have something to give, that you possess something someone else needs, it will do wonders for your self-esteem.

The closest neighbors to you or me are the members of our families. Earlier I discussed the role of negative influences on a person's self-esteem, and how positive communication can build a person up. Try doing thoughtful things for your husband and your children. Don't neglect them while serving others. Take care of your family with love, and then move on to caring relationships. Encouragement is biblical, and we are instructed to do this daily.

Learn how to pay compliments—sincere ones. Start with members of your own family and you will find it easier to compliment others later on. I read this statement: "I never knew a blasé man whose face did not change when he heard that some action or creation of his had been praised." I don't care how "all together" people seem to be, they love it. Mark Twain said, "I can go for two months on one good compliment." I believe I could go three! When you begin to dislike people, do something nice for them. It is amazing what it does for the relationship.

In the book *Irregular People*, the author talks about individuals in your life you *have* to be around. Ordinarily, if you don't like someone, you stay clear of him. However, there are those with whom we must associate. Maybe it is a boss, a working associate, a family member you see at reunions or family gatherings, but you can't stand them. This book helped me. The main premise is that the person with a personality problem is *handicapped* just as surely as if he had a broken leg or broken arm. The handicap could be the result of something in his past he never took time to straighten out.

A second premise of the book is that such people are *not* likely to change. If we can be objective and change our attitudes toward them, it may help us. Often that can best be accomplished when we do something for them. For instance, pray for them. It is amazing how that will affect your attitude. You will have people in your church you will not like, or other people who continually irritate you. Don't let this be a problem for you. The old expression "kill them with kindness" is the best advice I can give. Do something for them—I really believe it will help you feel better and improve relations.

One affirmer was described as being "one of those people who keeps blowing up balloons despite the fact that this world is full of people with sharp needles." Are you that kind of person? Don't let other people dictate your behavior, but take charge of your own life. Minister to those you like and those you don't like.

I recently found a little book that belonged to my father. It is entitled *How to Solve Your Problems*. It is based on Scripture and I want to pass some of its wisdom on to you. The author suggests that we learn the "principle of good." According to this principle, doing a good turn generates its own rewards—it brings goodness to you. You don't wait in vain for someone to return your favor. You can expect satisfaction simply by being good yourself.

That principle has helped me. Good + good = good. If you keep doing good, keep spreading joy and encouragement, you may not get strokes back from the person you helped, but you *will* get them.

Isn't it wonderful to be around encouraging and affirming people? Then apply the principle of good whether individuals deserve it or not, whether you like them or not, and I guarantee you it will improve your self-image.

I've heard that the words *encouragement* and *Holy Spirit* come from the same root word. The Holy Spirit is the one called alongside of us as a helper, a comforter. When we are in that helping capacity, we are closer to doing the work of the Holy Spirit than at any other time. Are you an encourager?

I don't know anything that has given the cause of Christ or the Lord a bad name like Christians who don't act like Christians and who don't behave in a way to bring honor to the Savior. Do you know what *glorify* means? *Glorify* means to "enhance the reputation of." When you glorify Jesus, you are enhancing *His* reputation. Isn't that what we want to do? We want to do it by our dress, our personality, and our service. We want to do it by a loving attitude toward other people. Promote others. It is the best way in the world to build self-esteem, and to minister.

Joyce Landorf wrote about basement people and balcony people.

Balcony people are the encouragers. That concept comes from the book of Hebrews, reminding us we are surrounded by a great cloud of witnesses. When I read that passage, I can always see people who have gone to be with the Lord cheering me on as I run the race of life. When we are encouraging others, we are being balcony people to them.

Basement people, on the other hand, are those who drag you down. Are there some people who have that negative effect on you? These people are incapable of giving compliments. If they do, why is it so often a backhanded one, such as, "You look nice . . . since you lost weight"? People who can't give complements are basically insecure. To build their self-estem, they downgrade others, and if they do say something positive, it often carries a critical undertone. I don't enjoy being around such persons. As I warned in chapter 2, "Don't traffic with a pessimist." Even though you may want to help those with this mind-set, don't stay around them long enough to be influenced, especially if you have a tendency in that direction anyway. I, for one, don't need the influence of basement people. Be a balcony person, and you will find others will want to be around you and you will bring great honor to our Lord.

Try to recall when you last gave encouragement. How long has it been since you gave someone a "face-lift" or elevated someone's spirit? How long has it been since you said, "I love you," "I appreciate you," "I am so glad you are my friend," or "I am sorry"? It is not always easy.

I grew up a spoiled brat. I was the last of five children, and I had pretty much anything I wanted. I had never said "I'm sorry" until I married. It is still hard for me, but I've learned that things heal. My son said to me once, "Mother, just remember all hurts don't bleed!" Practice affirming others. If you will set a goal of giving five compliments a day, you will soon become an encourager. But remember that we need encouragement too. This is a two-way street, and rest assured we are going to need help at some point. These truths are self-evident:

> Every human needs someone sometime.
> Everyone needs to be needed.
> Everyone has a gift someone else needs.

In the North every May 1, there is a tradition of taking baskets of flowers to people as a sign of friendship. This serves as a reminder that everyone needs flowers—and appreciation—sometime. That is a custom we all would do well to adopt.

The personal touch is what we are after. People must know they are important, and have special significance. Assure them God loves them and so do you. The most noticeable thing about Jesus is His interest in individuals. Great crowds followed Him, but He always took time to love, heal, and bless individuals. In our computerized society I find the personal touch desperately needed.

I agree with the one who said, "To leave a mark on others around me and following me which will point them to God is my greatest desire." Share anything positive you can. When you go to the grocery store, look for something to affirm in the one who checks you out, or the person who sacks your groceries. I hope you have a positive influence in the beauty shop or in your classroom. Anything positive you know about your neighbor, verbalize it.

We know how we want to be loved. We just have to turn around and love somebody else that same way. That is a good rule of thumb. If you really want to be happy, try praising people. It works every time. Proverbs 14:22 says, "Those who *plan* good be granted mercy and quietness!"

Using Your Gifts

Promote others in your own unique way, using your own spiritual gifts. I don't know anything that has liberated student wives any more than a study of their gifts.

I teach a class first term especially for the new student wives, who are just coming in with their husbands. I have everything from the high school graduate to the one who has completed a masters degree. We have the whole spectrum. Many are second-career people. They have been in other fields of service for years and have now been called to ministry.

As you might imagine, I get a lot of student wives who are uptight about their roles. They have heard all the expectations. I know how they feel, because I had heard those same expectations. I married into this family of preachers, and there had never been a preacher in my family. I knew the Lord and I was active in church, but I didn't know very much about ministers or being a minister's wife. I can identify with those who are nervous about their responsibilities.

When we talk about gifts, I tell them on the front end, you don't have to do it all. They have grown up thinking this. Of course, in many small churches you do end up doing a lot of things whether you are gifted or not. However, understanding how God has gifted all of us, though not in the same area, takes off the pressure. I always tell the student wives that I am the only preacher's wife anyone ever heard of who can't play the piano. One young girl came up to me after class once and asked, "Mrs. Leavell, you mean I don't have to know how to play the piano?" I said no and she was relieved. She thought she had found a friend.

One of my students, after we had this discussion about gifts, went to a country church where her husband was supply preacher. A sweet lady asked her immediately upon arrival, "Do you play the piano?" I always tell my students they can reply *anything* if they show their teeth. Just smile and say, "No, I don't play the piano." This student followed the advice that I had given her, which settled the issue until she came back Sunday night and was asked to play again. She smiled and said, "No, I *still* don't play the piano." We have had a lot of good laughs over this. Have you been liberated from the feeling of having to do it all? Hopefully, a study of your gifts will help you find that special place of service only you can fill.

Our salvation is the beginning point of our spiritual giftedness. The Holy Spirit gives these gifts at the moment of conversion, and then it is up to us to take possession of our possession. We must unwrap these individual gifts within us, and win and promote others through the use of them.

What are gifts? We have all received them at Christmas, birthdays, or maybe Mother's Day. A gift is an item given as an expression of love to a significant person. What are spiritual gifts? They are given to us by God. We could not have acquired or obtained any of them. A spiritual gift is not something you purchase or work for. It is something given to you, a significant person, out of love by our Heavenly Father.

People often say, "Me? Me, a gifted child? On a scale of one to ten, I am a minus four. When He passed out the gifts, I was behind the door. I don't have any gifts." I went through life making that statement. You have heard the saying, "jack of all trades, and master of none." That was the way I felt. But when we say, "I don't have any gifts," we are contradicting the very Word of God.

In 1 Corinthians 12:4, it reminds us:

> Now there are diversities of gifts, but the same Spirit. And there are differences of administrations, but the same Lord. And there are diversities of operations, but it is the same God which worketh all in all.

Right there we are told there are diversities and differences, but then the seventh verse says, "But the manifestation of the Spirit is given to every man to profit withal." That includes every man, woman, boy, and girl. Gifts, though they are different, are given to every single one of us. Our salvation is a free gift, and these spiritual gifts, or grace gifts, are also free. We don't deserve them, and we don't choose them. If I had been choosing my gift, what do you think I would have chosen? Right—to be able to play the piano!

There has never been a church that had enough pianists. Actually, when you start out in country churches, it is a help if you can play. Our son was pastor at Delcambre, Louisiana. He was a seminary student and single. The first Sunday five people arrived for services; they ended up several years later with fifty or sixty in the congregation. But there was no one to play the piano. Our son had grown up in the sixties and could play the guitar, so he accompanied the congregational hymns on that guitar. Now it wasn't the most orthodox service you ever saw, but that was the best they could do. I coached him when he was looking for a wife, advising, "Honey, find out early on if she can play the piano."

But we don't pick our gifts. Verse 11 of 1 Corinthians states, "... and He gives them to each one, just as He determines." As God wills, He gifts us. We are saved by grace, we grow by grace, and we are endowed by grace. Gifts are bestowed on Christians for serving the Lord.

The church thrives on the harmonious functioning of all the parts of the body. Our different gifts all fit together to make this harmony possible. We depend on each member to minister effectively to others through his or her giftedness.

These gifts are not given just to adorn us or for personal display, but to use for Him to promote others. Our gifts are extensions of His hands in the world as we minister for Him. We are as vital to His program as Abraham or Moses were. We read about those Old Testament patriarchs who were called and make no association whatsoever with our call for service today. What about Esther in the Scriptures, who came to the "kingdom for such a time as this"? We need to add our names to the roll call of the faithful. God has written our names in history.

How are we going to involve ourselves in carrying out the story of redemption? Many today are interested in "finding themselves." I'm more interested in what you are going to do *after* you find yourself! How are you going to relate your gifts, your abilities, to making a difference in this world? Ask yourself how you are living out your area of service and responsibility.

In her book *Giftedness: Discovering Your Areas of Strength,* Marcia L. Mitchell discusses some specific gifts and how they promote others:

> ENCOURAGING quickly gathered the children around her and concentrated on memorizing scripture verses with them.
>
> MERCY held the children in her lap and kissed their skinned knees, paying attention to a handicapped child.
>
> After class, ADMINISTRATION placed the chairs in precise rows, reorganized the supplies cabinet, and created a more efficient attendance record book.
>
> GIVING spent her time deciding how many new tables and chairs the room needed and calculated the cost of a new carpet and paint job, quietly making plans to pay for it herself.
>
> SERVING kept the children supplied with crayons and paper, noted two children who needed new shoes, and made arrangements with GIVING to help paint the room on Saturday.
>
> TEACHING took a small group of children to one corner of the room after their lesson and helped them apply the Bible story to their own lives.
>
> PROPHECY knelt beside the chair of one child who really had a question about sin. She carefully explained the difference between right and wrong.

We all shine in some areas—maybe your strength lies in giving, serving, or teaching. Find out what you have to give and share it with others.

What God has given to us personally, we must discover personally. No one can do this for you. No one could accept Christ for you, and no one can find your gift for you. Others may help, but we must find our areas of giftedness by personal discovery. When we do, it is the most exciting thing imaginable. Serving is no longer a chore, something we've *got* to do. We find a joy that a lot of people have never found in service.

I can speak from both sides of the fence. When we first married, I was a Christian, but had grown very little in my faith. I wasn't about to do all of those things expected of preachers' wives. I'm not proud of this, but I can remember telling Landrum, "You can just tell that pulpit committee they are not getting two staff members for the price of one." I might add that more preachers have been ruined by misfit wives than have been ruined by sin and the devil. I *missed the blessing* for many years. What little I did was because I had to.

I've got a long way to go, but I have made progress. Now I want to do more than time will permit, because I have discovered my gifts. There is just no comparing my joy today to those early days. Of course, I still don't try to do everything, but I do try to make use of all the gifts I have.

This change in my attitude did not come overnight, and did not come from any external influence or person. No one can make this change for us. My husband, my mother-in-law, nor any other preacher's wife could have done this for me. Only God could. *Service comes out of our relationship with Him.* It is the overflow that blesses others. He helped me find my spiritual gifts, and I know if He can change my attitude from negative to positive, He can do the same for you.

I was in a bookstore one time and saw a book entitled *How to be a Preacher's Wife and Love It.* I took it to the cashier and commented, "I don't know how I could enjoy it any more, but I want to see what somebody else says." She said, "Oh, we sell *lots* of these. Men come in and buy it for their wives!" It's sad, because those men can't really help their wives find their own joy. As Anne Morrow Lindbergh says, "A woman must come of age by herself."

That is also true for men or other members of the family. There are many women who would love for their husbands to be more spiritual. The discovery of gifts must be personal for him also, but oh, what joy when we find that right place of service and can get to work in promoting others. Susannah Wesley said, "I am content to fill a little space if God be glorified, but I want to fill that little space well."

Gifts and Talents

Now all people, believers and unbelievers, have talents or natural gifts that enable them to make a contribution to society. However, spiritual gifts are just for Christians. They are for believers only. A person who is not a Christian will not have spiritual gifts, but there are no ungifted believers.

What is the difference between talents and spiritual gifts? Much of the difference has to do with the way we use them. Talents are innate abilities frequently used selfishly, whereas gifts are "given to profit all." They are given for others, *never* to promote the self. Talents are abilities that come through genes and are developed through usage and education. Talents come at birth, but spiritual gifts come at *rebirth*. Gifts are those additional abilities, "something more" provided after a person becomes a Christian, to equip them to carry out specific functions within the body of Christ to minister effectively. This really has no relation to education. We sharpen them with education, but gifts are not dependent upon education.

Don't you know people who are not well educated yet make terrific contributions because the Lord gifted them? I have known those who could not even speak correct English but had the gift of teaching. There are godly deacons or women who have worked in the W.M.U. who did not have the blessing of education, but were gifted by any standard. Often gifts build on a natural foundation. Sometimes God gifts us in areas where we have a natural ability, but other times He gifts us in new and different ways.

My speaking in public is a gift. When I was in high school, I would tell my youth leader, "I will do anything if you just won't make me stand up and speak." I offered to make posters instead, and until you've seen my posters you cannot fully appreciate that! Public speaking is still hard for me, but there is no doubt in my mind God has given me the courage to try.

There are many, I'm afraid, who teach Sunday School when it is simply the fulfillment of a duty. There is a big difference between ministering your gift and doing a job. The difference between pastors who "work" and who are "called" is obvious. Occasionally I read an account of an interview with a minister who talks about when he "decided" to go into the ministry, and never mentions being called. This explains the difference. You can be gifted as a public speaker, and not be called to preach.

There is also a difference between exercising our gifts and busyness. Do you know those who are "busy" in the Lord's work, but they never find the joy of service? Landrum tells about a lady who called him one day and said, "Dr. Leavell, I have *got* to have a job down at the church." The background of that story was that her daughter had run away and married. She was an only child, and they had such high hopes for her. The mother and daddy were devastated. The mother said, "I have got to have a job down at the church or I am going to go crazy." Now was that a motivation for kingdom service? I don't think so.

When I speak of ministry, I am referring to something far more than what one well-known preacher's wife had in mind. She had been chided by her husband for not being more deeply involved. Her defense to those of us gathered was, "I have a ministry. I take his shirts to the cleaners every Monday and pick them up every Friday." That may be part of the necessary care we give our husbands, but I think Jesus and Paul must have had more than that in mind when they said "feed My sheep" and "neglect not the gift that is within you."

I remember well the first time I was ever asked to teach. The teacher was going to be away and asked me if I would fill in for her. I turned her down. It bothered me so much that I promised the Lord if she ever asked me again, I would do it. She did, and I did.

The first adult class I accepted was a class of unmarried women aged twenty-one to twenty-four. I lasted six months. I then took on a class of married women of the same age group, and absolutely *loved* it. You ask, what was the difference? I don't know, but it was the beginning of my love affair with young marrieds. That was *my* spot. My point is you can be busy and not find fulfillment. When you find the area God has prepared for *you*, all I can tell you is you will know it. Few things are more important than knowing and using your gifts.

I would suggest you "pore over" the biblical lists of gifts. Examine and evaluate these knowing that, as you do, you will begin to see yours. "God in heaven appoints each man's work" (John 3:27).

The churches Landrum and I have served have given me all the freedom in the world to be *me*. I have never felt restricted in how or where I have chosen to minister, but I *have* served. The only ministers' wives I hear criticized are those who do nothing. Try on all the gifts and minister yours faithfully.

Think about what you do best. What do you enjoy doing and what do other people compliment you on? Listen to the response of people because gifts are seldom discovered in complete isolation. These could be good indicators of your giftedness.

Above all, don't be afraid to explore and try new things. Experiment with various responsibilities. You can start where you are with opportunities that are at hand. There is nothing like a new challenge to stir your blood. Keep your eyes open to needs around you and plug in with the inclination of your heart. God will confirm your gifts and build your self-image as you put Him first, serving and promoting others faithfully. *Don't miss this blessing.*

PART III

The Reality of the Present

CHAPTER 5

LOOK AROUND:
Paint the House

THE THIRD STEP I WOULD suggest for improving your self-image is to "paint the house." As someone has stated, "If you know your body is the temple of the Holy Spirit, you might do well to paint the house!" So far we have been examining the importance of looking back and looking within, but taking care of how we appear to those outside of us is also helpful for our self-esteem. I probably should have put "painting the house" first, not so much because of its importance, but because nothing will bring such immediate results. So here I will examine four aspects of looking your best: its purpose, its expression of your personality, taking care of your person, and your "packaging."

The Purpose of a Good Appearance

C. S. Lovett calls the body an "earth suit." Someone else suggested, "Your body is the flesh that clothes His presence." Our bodies are the earthly dwelling places for the Spirit of God. A sloppy, unkempt exterior is a dead giveaway for low self-esteem and faith. People who like themselves take good care of themselves. The Scripture says in Hebrews 12 that we are "to present our bodies as a living sacrifice, wholly acceptable unto God." We cannot present to Him what we don't own. In that sense we have to possess our bodies, and then give them back to Him to use as He sees fit. The purpose of all this is to glorify Him.

Remember this statement: "Any ridicule that falls upon you will fall in great measure upon the cause you represent." What does that say to us as Christian women, and even as ministers' wives? If we do not do our best in appearance, then we are not going to be very good advertisements for our faith, are we? Our negligence will reflect upon the cause we represent, and we represent the Lord Jesus and His church.

We must take our appearance seriously. Ministers' wives especially are visible people. We stand before our congregation. People expect the preacher and his wife to dress acceptably. If we don't, we are saying something about our faith and our Lord. As Christians we are called to excellence, and that includes a first-class appearance. If we feel that we look good, we'll act with confidence.

I am not in the pastorate any longer. I am a member who is "observing," and I do want to be proud of my preacher's wife when I introduce her to my friends. I also want to take pride in my own appearance, and in the other women in my church.

There are individuals who think it is unspiritual to talk about appearance. I am quick to say, "Not so." As Christians we ought to be the best advertisements possible of our faith. Do you give the impression that you think it is unspiritual to be interested in your appearance? If so, an impression is all that it is. Such a feeling simply is not our nature. Most women were *born* interested in their appearance. For Christians this must not be just a desire to call attention to the self, but an earnest desire to bring honor to Jesus. We need to be the very best we are capable of being. We cannot all be beautiful, but we can all be neat, clean, and dress in keeping with our personalities. There is nothing unspiritual about that. As a matter of fact, I think it is unspiritual if we don't care, or if we don't do anything to enhance His "earth suit" or His "dwelling place."

Expressing Your Personality

Let's move on from purpose to *personality*. A personality is the sum total of individual characteristics. Each one of us is unique. Our personalities have been shaped by heredity and various life experiences. We manifest our personalities in our actions, speech, and emotions. We are all different, so don't lower yourself to being a carbon copy. There is a song entitled, "The One and Only You." We are custom-designed individuals "fearfully and wonderfully made"

(Psalm 139:14). We are divine originals—there is just one like me and just one like you. I think I latched on to that concept because I have never had an original anything. One day I woke up to the fact that I myself am an original, and that is exciting!

I made that statement in my seminary class one night and the next day, as I walked across campus, one of our students waved and yelled to me. He called, "Mrs. Leavell, I hear I am married to a divine original."

Yes, we are unique. We have to figure out, in this pursuit of who we are, what our personalities are. What are the things that have come into our lives and made us the way we are? When we understand our personalities, then we dress accordingly. In other words, what message do you wish to convey to others about you? Find your personal style. Don't just dress like others. Determine who you are, and look good within your own style.

Do you encounter people who obviously don't care about their appearance? There are people on our campus who have given little attention to God's temple. They have neglected to dress it up or clean it up. They tell me by their appearance that they are unconcerned about physical improvement. I think as Christian women we need to tell the world we care. Our bodies are God's temple, and we need to paint the house. Don't settle for just looking lovely. Do it based on who you are and the message you want to convey.

Taking Care of Your Person

Let's give attention now to your *person*. There are practical tools by which every woman can capture the beauty which is rightfully hers. I know most of you have little money, so I want to tell you five things to enhance your appearance that are *free*.

The first impression we make on others is usually created nonverbally through the way we walk, our posture. We are saying something to the world through our posture about how we envision ourselves. If you have a low self-image, your natural tendency is to hold your head down and slump! Hold your shoulders up, your head high, and remind yourself, "I am somebody, I am a divine original, I was born in His image, and Jesus has saved me." As you tell yourself these things, I believe it will make you stand a little straighter and a little taller. Proverbs 23:7 says, "For as a man thinketh in his heart, so is he. . . ." Your body talks and the world has become expert in reading that language. What is your body saying?

Marge Caldwell recommends picturing a string going all the way through your body and coming out the top of your head. If you pull on that string, everything is going to come up.

I remember when Marge came to our church for the first time. Ann, our daughter, was a teenager. I was constantly telling her, "Hold your shoulders up!" It was as if Marge had overheard one of those conversations because she was emphatic in saying, "Never tell anyone to hold their shoulders up. That is an unnatural position. Encourage them to raise their diaphragm, and the shoulders will automatically come up." Try it. Raise your diaphragm, pull on that string, and see if you don't feel more confident. Good posture will take years off your looks. If you want to "lose" ten pounds, this is the best way to do it. Stretching out your midriff makes you look less heavy. Practice good posture. It is the backbone of confidence and charm.

The second free improvement to your person is a smile. Of all the things you wear, your expression is the most important. Nothing will make as much difference in the impression you leave as the expression on your face. As they say, "You are never fully dressed without a smile."

Consider these statements about a smile:

"When you smile at someone you automatically make them feel better. They in turn will smile at someone else and you have begun a chain reaction."

"It is impossible to make somebody else feel better and not feel better yourself."

"If you meet someone too tired to smile, leave one of yours. Nobody needs a smile as much as those who have none to give."

"Some people grin and bear it, others smile and change it."

"There are hundreds of languages in the world, but a smile speaks all of them." Do you remember the song Sandy Patti made famous entitled, "Love in Any Language"? A smile expresses affection in any language.

"Nothing is more beautiful than cheerfulness in an old face."

"A smile is free, but gives much." Practice a smile whether you feel like it or not. It is the best thing you can do.

A third way to enhance your appearance is to use eye contact. Your eyes are the most important tools in nonverbal communication. They are indeed "windows of the soul." Look people in the eye. People with a poor self-image usually look at the floor, or the ceiling—*anywhere* but in your eyes.

Making eye contact lets others know you are talking to them and it says you are an important person. If this is not comfortable for you, practice on children. They are not going to tell anybody. Another good place to practice is in the line on Sunday morning for greeting the new members. Look those persons right in the eye when you shake their hands. They are going to believe you are glad to see them. Eye contact sends one of the most powerful messages you and I can make about ourselves. You are saying not only that you are a person over there, but I am a person over here.

Love is best communicated through the eyes. Lovers have done this forever. Do you remember when your husband first looked at you, and when you first looked back at each other across the room? All kinds of signals can be sent through the eyes. I've heard it called "eyetact." If you practice this, you are well on the way to an improved self-image.

The fourth thing I would recommend is exercise. I know that is a dirty word, but you can do it for free. Staying in good physical condition not only adds years to your life, but life to your years. Are you familiar with the name Ken Cooper? He is the one who started the aerobics craze. He is a medical doctor who heads a well-known fitness clinic in Dallas. He was on our campus several years ago, speaking primarily to preachers. He looked out at them and said, "You may want to get the gospel out to the ends of the earth, but if you don't take care of your bodies you may not have the vehicle to get it there." I'll never forget that statement. Emerson reminded us, "The first wealth is health."

John W. Drakeford, in *The Awesome Power of the Healing Thought*, outlines the benefits of exercise thus:

> Exercise may be the closest thing we have to a panacea for the ills that beset the human frame. It is the prescription without medicine, the mood elevator without drugs, the pickup without a hangover, the weight control without the diet, the cosmetics found in no drug store, the sedative without a chemical, the

tranquilizer without a pill, the indicator of life without a cardio-
gram, the therapy more effective than any psychiatrist's couch, the
cure for depression without a fee, the fountain of youth without a
legend.

And yet, with all these great incentives, fewer than 20 percent of
American women exercise regularly!

I don't know how you feel about exercise, but whether you like
it or not, you need to do it. You need to encourage your husband
to exercise regularly and to take care of God's temple. Ken Cooper's
advice was to get our heart beat up to capacity and keep it there for
twenty to thirty minutes. This can be done best with four exercises:
walking, jogging, bicycling, or swimming. We can touch our toes,
and firm up our muscles, but that is not helping the heart. There
must be rigorous activity to condition the heart.

We are joggers at our house. I don't tell you that in order to
straighten my halo. I tell you that because I *despise* jogging. My
husband tells me frequently, "Honey, if I hated it as bad as you do,
I would quit." I say, "No, I'm too mean to quit. Call me anything but
a quitter." I am not going to quit, but I don't like it. I go early in the
morning because if I wait, I can talk myself out of it. When I tell
people this, they look at me and ask, "Oh, but don't you feel better?"
No, I don't feel better! I feel good all the time anyway. I only feel
better because I know I have done what is right.

Here is the formula:

DO right because it
IS right until it
FEELS right.

It feels right for me when I am sitting on my front porch drinking
my second cup of coffee and I am *through*.

I didn't jog for years and Landrum did. I finally decided he was
going to be on his second wife if I didn't do something. I couldn't
stand the thought of that, so I decided I better get out there with
him. *Do something* for physical exercise. Walking is fine. The only
advantage jogging has over walking is that you can do it faster, and
I am always in a hurry.

Pick out something that fits your personality and your life-style.
Don't jog because I jog. That may not suit you but *do something*. Get

on a program of walking, jogging, swimming, or bicycling—anything that will keep your body in shape.

The body is a remarkable machine, and you need to take care of it. People think if you jog you are going to automatically lose ten to twenty pounds. Not so. I don't know if I have ever lost a pound jogging. Of course, I sometimes wonder what I might look like if I didn't jog!

The body is God's temple. Most of us have let it go to pot. Good grooming really begins with good habits, but changing habits takes time, effort, and patience. I can remember when I first jogged I could not run two blocks. I thought I would *never* get to the end of the street. When I finally made it, I thought I would *never* turn around and head back. It takes time—I'm told it takes thirty days—to develop a habit of exercise. Maybe you need to walk for thirty days, jog for thirty days, or ride a bicycle until it becomes a way of life. Take care of the temple.

When we lived in Wichita Falls, our church had a recreational facility where Landrum had a daily workout. He ran a mile in the gym at noon and then usually played a game of volleyball with the guys. Our snack bar served a light lunch, and he would shower, dress, and go back to work. For him that was a good schedule. I remember him saying many times, "You know, honey, I really did not have time to exercise today, but that may be the most spiritual thing I do." Taking care of our bodies simply means we can operate for a longer number of years.

It is never too late to change your pattern. God gives us the free will to choose our own life-styles. I keep throwing out the words "choose" and "choice" because it is up to you. Be a good advertisement for the Lord. We have a lot of advertisements that are not so hot. If there is anything that I would like to be, it is a good witness for the Lord. One of the ways that we can do that is by taking care of our bodies through exercise.

The fifth freebie is diet. I don't really want to talk about this. I gained ten pounds on a recent vacation at the beach. I knew I was doing it, so I planned to go home and lose it. Guess what? Since then I still haven't lost a pound. It is hard to preach self-control when you've not practiced it. Diet is another dirty word, but weight control is something most of us need to work at all the time. What is your comfortable weight? Small people often say, "I need to lose five pounds." I want to swat them and say, "Hush." However, I have finally learned that if you are small, five pounds can make you just as uncomfortable as my ten is making me or your twenty is making you.

What is your frame? I have operated all my life under the delusion that I had a large frame. I would convince myself I could carry a little extra weight because I was big-boned and tall. Guess what? I found out how you determine your frame, and I don't have a large frame. I always said the only little part about me is my wrist. This is one way you determine if your frame is small, medium, or large. My wrist indicates I actually have a small frame, so I have misguided myself all these years.

We also need to be apprised of the troublemaker foods and how to monitor our eating habits. I joined a dieting program once, and lost twenty-two pounds. The one thing I learned in all of those support sessions was you could really lose weight if you practiced portion control. That means no second helping and decent-sized portions.

If you seem unable to practice that life-style, don't hesitate to get help. If you need a weight-loss group for support, join one. My son-in-law is going now to an Overeaters Anonymous group. I'm proud of him for recognizing his need for help. These meetings help you change poor eating habits. You learn about food exchanges and what constitutes a healthy diet. If you have ever had a family member who was a diabetic, you know about bread, protein, fruit, and milk exchanges. Balanced meals need food from these four groups. Somebody said, "Poor nutrition can be a cause of weak willpower." If you are not eating nutritious foods, you will feel hungry and substitute junk food. We are raising a generation of junk-food eaters. Our kids would rather have french fries from McDonald's than a meal anytime. It is up to you and me to provide meals that are nutritious.

Landrum and I have been on every diet imaginable at one time or another. He says we have lost a thousand pounds—just not at the same time! I have found you cannot lose weight the same way twice. It seems dieting must have a new twist to keep you diligent.

Sweets are my *big* problem. I eat to get to the dessert! I couldn't stand the thought of cutting out all sweets, so not long ago I decided to cut down and only have a dessert once a week. Now that was not a new decision, but always before I had made it *any* day of the week. This week Tuesday, next week Thursday, and then the next week it would be Tuesday and Thursday. I'm good at doing that.

This time I settled on Friday night. Regardless of what is going on or where we go, I get no desserts until Friday. This has worked for me, and even my friends now know my dessert night. If you need to lose ten pounds, try it. It gives you something to look forward to, and believe me I don't waste those calories on any dessert that's not *wonderful*.

Gimmicks won't work. To lose weight and keep it off, you must change your entire approach to eating. This means breaking old habits and learning a new way of life. We must eat to live, not live to eat! This is tough because eating is one of the most fundamental pleasures of life. However, a new mind-set *can* be gained, and the results are enormously rewarding.

I know of one pulpit search committee who eliminated a man from consideration because they felt his obesity would reduce his effectiveness in their particular church. To many, this speaks of a lack of self-control which may indicate a spiritual problem.

Remember: slimmer bodies look younger and age more gracefully. I understand there is more to life than the absence of fat, but losing excess weight will add years to your life and build self-esteem. Pay attention to your posture, your smile, your eyes, your exercise, and your diet. All of these are free.

Your Packaging

The way you look affects how you feel about yourself, so let's consider your *packaging*. The way you dress and do your hair and makeup tells much about your self-image and influences how other people react to you. Someone said, "People will take you at your own self-appraisal. If you put a small value upon yourself, you can rest assured the world will not raise the price!" We send powerful messages with our hairstyles, makeup, and clothes.

As wives and mothers, we so often neglect ourselves because of busy homemaking responsibilities. This is a carry-over from the past. I was brought up to believe Mother was the self-sacrificing member of the family. Mother didn't ever have any new clothes. She should never spend money on herself, but give it to her children. If anyone had to do without, she was the one. My own mother told me when I married a preacher, "Jo Ann, if it ever comes to the place that either you or Landrum has to do without clothes, be sure it is you. I have seen enough seedy preachers to last me a lifetime!" That was her evaluation of the ministers she knew.

Something that helped me overcome the reluctance to spend money on myself is that I learned the distinction between poise and charm:

> Poise is when you feel at ease.
> Charm is when you make someone else feel at ease.

My contention is you are not likely to think of others until *you* are poised and feel at ease with yourself. This ease often comes when some care is given to your appearance. Let me illustrate. Have you ever changed clothes several times on Sunday morning and left for church feeling less than your best? Surely you have. When you arrived on those days, who were you thinking about? Right—you were totally absorbed with yourself.

On the other hand, if you plan well and give proper care and attention to your appearance, then you are able to concentrate on others. Do your best, but once you walk out the door, forget yourself and show interest in and concern for others.

Do you know how long you have to sell yourself to others? If you were going in for a job interview, you would have about six seconds to make that strong impression. Most of us are guilty of making snap judgments. Occasionally I change my mind, but too often my mind is made up based on a first impression. Hence the statement, "You never have a second chance to make a first impression."

In my seminary classes I always illustrate this principle with two identical boxes. Both are wrapped in the same white paper, and I stress the fact that they hold the exact same contents. The only difference is one of them is tied with colorful ribbon and a beautiful, big bow. Now if I was giving you a choice between these packages as a gift, which one would you choose? Right—and that pulpit committee will pick the pretty package too!

One student said she had trouble with the idea of selling herself to a committee. Life itself is a constant selling process, and our appearance is an important message we give the world. In fact, 90 percent of what people remember about us is communicated nonverbally. If we are untidy in appearance, we court disaster. I have certain information I have collected through the years from search committees. One such document lists ten things looked for in a preacher. Up close to the top of the list is personal appearance.

There has always been a distinction between the packaging and the product. I understand that the quality of life is more important than the appearance, but that should not negate the fact that the world needs to see we care about our bodies. It is never a question of either/or, but both/and. The Lord Who made you is concerned about your body, as well as your soul and spirit, and this includes your appearance.

Remember, looking good starts at the top. Your hair is the only accessory you wear all the time. It serves as a frame for your face, and we have to choose carefully what is right for the picture. Ask for advice. Most beauticians are trained and know what looks best on a given person. Pick out someone whose hair looks the way you would like yours to look and ask them who cut it. Nothing will date you quicker than an out-of-style hairdo. The opposite of that is also true. A good haircut may be your best investment.

Caution: be careful of two things about hair as you age.

1) Color—God uses gray to soften lines and skin tones, and it can contribute to great beauty.

2) Length—Long hair is for the young. For those of us over forty, shoulder-length hair should be a thing of the past. It often accentuates age or points to a mid-life crisis.

The only advice I have about makeup is something I read recently. "Whatever you do shouldn't look like you did it!" Haven't you seen those who look for the world like they have on a Halloween mask? When makeup is that obvious, it is not done in good taste. All color should be applied sparingly and blended smoothly over a *clean* face.

Most cosmetics counters will give you a free facial, and show you how to highlight your best features and shadow those you do not want noticed. Accept the things that cannot be changed, but improve what you can. Take advantage of all help that is available, and above all, *stay up-to-date.*

Years ago, when my children were small, I remember reading in the newspaper that if you had not changed your lipstick color in the last year you were behind the times. At that moment I remember thinking mine had probably not been changed in ten years! I made my way to the store, related to the clerk what I had read, and came home with a new excitement as a result of a simple change.

Somewhere I read:

> At age twenty you have the face God gave you.
> At age forty you have the face you are working on.
> At age sixty you have the face you deserve.

What about your clothes? The average person, man or woman, wears 10 percent of his or her wardrobe 90 percent of the time. For those of us on a limited budget, my suggestion is to concentrate on that 10 percent and choose it with care. This involves wise planning, attention to color, and sensible and realistic goals for achieving the desired results.

Begin by doing a wardrobe analysis for every season. Try on everything in your closet, and determine what you want to wear again. I always enlist a friend or family member to do this with me. There are also professionals who do this for a nominal fee. Anything is more fun with company, plus it is hard for me to be objective when it comes to some of my past favorites. If you are unable to coordinate well, *ask for help.* You have numerous people in your church who would be flattered if asked to assist you.

I have always needed help accessorizing. I'm told 30 percent of your clothes budget ought to be put in accessories. They can be real budget stretchers, and can update old drab outfits like nothing else. Friends who had a flair in this regard have always come to my rescue. Now the Lord has given me *two* daughters-in-law who can help me accessorize. Isn't that just like the Lord to give us double blessings?

Make a list of what needs to be hemmed, altered, or replaced. Take this with you when you go shopping so you won't buy in a hit-or-miss manner. Buy only items which coordinate with what you have rather than isolated items. I'm sure we all have "white elephants" hanging in our closets we bought on impulse, but absolutely nothing to wear with them. When we do that, we are not getting the most mileage out of our wardrobe dollar.

Next, determine the color group and style that does the most for you. Take advantage of the color charts that have become readily available since the "Color Me Beautiful" craze. It took me twenty years, but I finally determined for myself what colors were best for *me*. You can give away over a period of time anything not becoming to you. Who knows—someone could share some clothes with you.

Fashions change, but I'm discussing style in the sense of what's good for *you*. Recognize your best features and buy clothing most flattering to your figure. Be realistic about your problem areas, and read up on what are "no-no's" for you. Don't call attention in your clothing to a line you do not want noticed or emphasized. For instance, I do *not* have a small waist so I seldom wear belts. Why would I want to call attention to what I don't have?! If you are on the heavy side, never wear a jacket that ends at your widest point. Darker colors and vertical lines will be best for you because they will lengthen and diminish your size. Try to use style deliberately to create the impression of a more proportioned figure.

Above all, wear clothing that fits properly. Dresses that are too tight will not only be uncomfortable, but will look cheap and make you look even larger. Ask yourself several questions before you buy a particular garment:

> Does this outfit go with my personality?
> Will it fit my life-style? Spend your fashion budget where you
>   spend your time.
> Do I have the figure to wear it?
> Will it go with clothes presently in my closet?

It has been well said that "learning to make your appearance work for you instead of against you is a skill that exemplifies being a good steward of what God has given you." Along with practicing the presence of God and promoting others, "painting the house" will improve your self-image. I hope you will use your appearance to play a more influential role in your life as a Christian, and don't miss the blessing.

CHAPTER 6

LOOK AROUND:
Husband-Wife Relationship

I SAT IN A CONFERENCE several years ago at Ridgecrest. The entire week was concerned with clergy marriages in trouble. Many of these marriages get in trouble at seminary level. Don't let that happen to you. Just because you are preparing for the ministry is no guarantee your marriage is invincible. The devil is not automatically going to leave you alone for three years or thirty years.

An experience John Sullivan related points this out. He said he always went to camp with his young people, and usually he spent the entire week trying to keep the young people apart. Then they married and he spent the rest of the time trying to keep them together! That's sad, isn't it? We are so excited to get married, and then we don't do what it takes to stay married. I am not going to give you a bunch of statistics because I'm sure you have heard them. They are depressing. Keep in mind that the statistics concerning marriage and divorce are for Christian *and* non-Christian marriages. We shouldn't take consolation in that fact, however, because Christian marriages are crumbling rapidly also.

In fact, a survey concluded, "Ministers are twice as likely to have marital problems than difficulties with their congregation." The same survey stated, "A pastor's wife is likely to find marital aggravations nearly TWICE as often as a pastor."

It used to be we never heard much about preachers getting divorced. We never heard about staff members with marriage

89

problems. Divorce was nonexistent for the deacons and Sunday School teachers in the church. Now it is commonplace. Even if we are committed to our mates, we get a little nervous when this is happening all around us. When neighbors and members of our Sunday School class are divorcing, it does bother us and affect us. We cannot avoid the fallout resulting from these problems because they have a way of impacting our lives and society.

What is the solution for the disintegration of the home? I believe it is marriage enrichment. I hope you will take advantage of every opportunity to go to retreats, marriage seminars, Ridgecrest, Glorieta—go anywhere you can to strengthen your marriage. We sometimes think these are just therapy sessions for sick marriages. Not so. These are growth experiences for healthy marriages. These minor tune-ups negate the need for a major overhaul. Isn't this what we want in our marriages? We want to grow as individuals and couples every day we live.

It is interesting that seven out of eight of the people seeking help in marriage are women. Anytime I have ever spoken to men on this subject, I remind them of that fact. Not long ago on campus we had a marriage enrichment retreat with Marge Caldwell. I was thrilled at the number of men who came along with their wives, because often they are slower to participate in things like that than women. There is just something about talking and thinking of love that keeps our marriages growing.

I am told 90 percent of our marriages are operating below their potential level. We *all* can improve. I don't care how good a marriage you have, it can be better. No matter how good my marriage is, it can stand improvement. I hope you see the need to work constantly at strengthening your relationship. A good marriage requires more than a ceremony and a shared bed.

Chuck Swindoll in *Strike the Original Match* says:

> A marriage is a lot like our house. While new it sparkles. Fresh smells, fun surprises, and new discoveries make each day snap, crackle, and pop. Sure, there's work to be done, but the newness takes away the hassle. As time passes, however, things change. Slowly, almost imperceptibly, the grit of responsibility mixed with the grind of routine starts to take its toll. Who hasn't experienced

it? Bills come due. Weeds sprout. Paint peels. Faucets drip. Drains clog. Floors lose their luster. Irritating tasks take place. The way we were turns into the way it is.

I don't care how newly married you are, you have probably already had to face bills and disagreements. There is something about routine that eats away at marriages. Landrum always asked, "What are you going to do when moonlight and roses turns to daylight and diapers?" It does not take long for that to happen, does it? Then we hear the voice of God reminding us, ". . . for better or worse, . . . till death do us part."

One definition of love is, "an unconditional commitment to an imperfect person." I hope you have committed yourself to the permanence of marriage and that divorce is never considered an option. Angel Martinez said he had never contemplated divorce, but frequently murder! All of us have been mad enough to kill our spouses, but we never thought of leaving them!

Early in our married life I told Landrum I would never leave. I don't think he was really worried about it, but I told him I would never let my daddy know I failed at anything, much less marriage. My father made it plain that when you married, *that was it!* There was never a door left open for you to return.

When Finis married our Ann, we told him up front, "Honey, she has absolutely no trade-in value!" You are supposed to *make* it work. If you need help, seek it. Talk to people who can advise you, but don't throw in the towel. Marriage is for keeps, and we must have that sort of determination.

According to the Bible, love has two aspects: *doing* and *enduring.* The enduring is this permanence we've talked about, but the doing is understanding a good marriage takes effort. My favorite passage of Scripture is the thirty-first chapter of Proverbs, where the ideal woman is described. If you read that account carefully, you will notice the action verbs: seeketh, riseth, girdeth, maketh, openeth, looketh. No wonder her husband praised her and her children rose up to call her blessed!

In countries where marriage is arranged, they look at it as a beginning. In our culture we look at marriage as an end. I am not suggesting we go back to the obsolete practice of arranged marriages, but we can learn something from them. We can view marriage as a time to *begin* making an effort. This is why I like the book title, *The Care and Feeding of a Happy Marriage*. It suggests activity.

Marriage enrichment has been likened to polishing fine silver. You must polish silver to keep it shiny and bright. Marriage must be polished with daily applications of interest, involvement, and love. Otherwise love will die through neglect. If we don't do our best to make it fall together, it may fall apart.

Let's take a look at several marital issues, and then see how we can keep our marriages strong. Communication is one of the most important issues of all in a marriage—so much so that I will devote an entire chapter to it a little later on. Some other important issues are the concept of marriage as a union of individuals, and the purposes of marriage—partnership, pleasure, and parenting. But before we can unite with a spouse, we must separate from our parents. We'll start there.

The Separation from Parents

As we are often advised, when all else fails read the instructions. Our instructions for marriage are found in Genesis 2:24. "Therefore shall a man leave his father and his mother, and shall cleave unto his wife: and they shall be one flesh." That is the divine sequence. We leave Father and Mother and cleave to this new partner. This severance is normal and depends on two things. It depends on the willingness of parents to let you go and it depends on your going. I hope you as parents will let your children go.

Girls often have a harder time than boys at making the transition. We have a tendency to call on daddy or look to daddy rather than this new husband for leadership. However, I made that shift *before* we were married. We were engaged and I had a wreck on my way to practice teach. I looked away and hit the car in front of me. Landrum still laughs because I called him before I called my daddy. But still, leaving my parents for this new life of marriage was a tough and sometimes frightening transition for me. Every bride knows what I mean.

And as for letting your own children go to their new mates, I can tell you this is not the easiest thing you will do. I am an old mother hen. I have always said I would love to live like they do on "Dallas," where I live in the big house and my family lives all around me. That would suit me just fine. I love my family and I love them close by. However, I know that is not God's plan. We are told that the time will come when our children will leave, just as we did.

In the pastorate Landrum always gave couples premarital counseling. When our daughter married I was so afraid he wouldn't feel this was necessary, but I insisted. I told him, "I want you to talk to Ann and Finis. I want you to tell them everything that you have ever told any other couple." I saw to it that they set up an appointment.

When the day arrived, they stayed in his office for what seemed like an eternity. I would have given *anything* to be a fly on the wall. I thought, "What in the world is he telling them that's taking so long?" I was dying to know.

Ann came in the door and asked, "Momma, guess what Daddy said?" I replied, "Tell me quick." "He said this is not my home anymore." What had he done? He had verbalized what the Bible calls severance. She was leaving to establish another home. She has visited often but never as a permanent resident.

We need to let our children go. The kindest thing you can do for your children is to take your hands *off* of their marriages. That is not easy either. It is not in my nature to keep my mouth shut. I don't know how successful I have been, but I try. Let them go; untie the apron strings. This is transition time. Marital bonding can only take place without outside interference. Your children won't love you less because they leave. Understand that marriage requires this transition from one life to another—you did it and so will they. If you make this transition fully, and allow your children to make it fully, then everyone's marriages will be that much stronger!

The Union with a Spouse

Matthew says, "Wherefore they are no more twain, but one flesh. What therefore God hath joined together, let not man put asunder." Marriage is basically a union. We leave and we cleave, and the idea in this word is that of being glued or bonded together.

I'm not too smart, but I have figured out all by myself why Jesus was so against divorce. When you separate one flesh, you are going to leave scars. God has promised to forgive but He never said He would remove the scars.

Some resist bonding because they feel it will rob them of their identity. When we are glued or welded together, we don't become like two liquids poured together in an indistinguishable mass. We still maintain our identity but we are just related in a new way. I've heard, "Marriage is not really marriage when it completely drains one for the sake of the other. It ought to enlarge both." Isn't this what we are to do? We ought to drain off the worst, enhance the best, and enlarge each other. It has been suggested, "Love is a commitment to making another person great." Is that your purpose in marriage? We should find delight in making our husbands feel their best. We have that capability.

Christian marriage at its best is a merger of two ministries. I hope you don't look at the ministry as belonging solely to your husband. I trust you had a ministry before you met him and will continue to minister all your life.

Our oldest son was thirty when he finally married. I thought we were never going to unload that kid on anyone! I really became concerned when I learned what he was looking for in a wife. He said, "Momma, I just want a fine Christian girl who could qualify for the Dallas Cowboy cheerleaders!" When I suggested I wasn't sure the Lord was making that kind anymore, he came back with the statement, "If He can create the world in six days, that is no hill to climb!"

Well, he found her at a youth camp where he was acting as camp pastor. I had prayed for a wife for him who had her own walk with the Lord. Lan had brought home a lot of cute girls, but none who I felt were "helpmate" material. Susanne was participating in that camp with the girls in her junior high Sunday School class. She was extremely active in her church in Florence, Alabama, and had taken vacation time from her job to be there. I'd say my prayer was definitely answered for a "merger of two ministries."

A tree makes a good model for marriage. The trunk of the tree represents our life together. We come together and form this solid source and then flower in different directions. Landrum and I do many things together, but not everything. I'm not involved every time he travels to preach nor is he involved every time I teach. We minister in different ways, but always with the support and help of the other. Much of my time and energy has centered in the home raising four children. This was an agreed-upon goal, and one which we feel has paid rich dividends.

Landrum and I met when I was a senior in high school. He came to my church soon after he arrived in New Orleans to enter the New Orleans Seminary. Dr. Roland Q. Leavell was president at that time, and his daughter, Dottie, introduced Landrum to me. Because I was young and he was a *big* graduate student, it took me awhile to get his attention. He was dating Newcomb girls, and I thought he was the most conceited guy I had ever met. In fact, I told Dottie, "I would love to date Landrum Leavell, get him wrapped around my little finger, and then drop him so quick it would make your head swim!" *His* version of that is I asked for the first date!

We double-dated at the end of that summer, a week before I went away to college. I had a date with his roommate. Some chemistry must have been set in motion that night because he asked me out the next night and every night thereafter until I left for Ward Belmont to attend school.

We didn't have the smoothest courtship. In fact, I remember well his call the morning I was to leave for Nashville. He said, "By the way, when you find out your new address, let me know and I *might* write you!" I told him, "Don't hold your breath!" My mother had always told me girls didn't make the first move, so I wasn't about to write first. He said, "No, I'm serious, let me know." I gave him the address I already knew, and waited and waited (not too patiently) for that first letter to arrive. We corresponded, called, and met whenever possible for the next four years until our marriage on July 28, 1953.

My big decision was whether I wanted to be a minister's wife, and his big one was whether or not I could adapt to that role. Our backgrounds, though both Christian, were poles apart in life-style. Lan, our oldest son, says frequently, "Dad, you know you really took a chance on Mom!" And that he did!

In fact, he delayed giving me a ring until I got a few things out of my system. I was scheduled to be a maid in the court of Rex, king of

Mardi Gras, that year. This included all day activities, a ball in the evening, a queen's supper, and all with an assigned escort. I got my engagement ring at eleven o'clock the next morning because, as he said, "Nobody is going to wear *my* ring and go out with somebody else!"

There are a lot of similarities between a salvation experience and marriage. Many of the same things take place. When we accept Christ as personal Savior, we commit our lives to one person. It is an exclusive relationship. When we marry, we commit ourselves to one person and our allegiance is transferred to our mate.

Another parallel is we go from one way of life to another. Before salvation we were making all the decisions. When we accept Christ, we do what He wants us to do. We have someone else to consider before making plans, setting goals, or choosing our life-styles. The same thing is true in marriage. We were single, did our own thing, and didn't have to ask anybody before spending money or establishing schedules. We did as we pleased, but now we have another person to consider, we are part of a *union*. We no longer make plans unilaterally. I read somewhere, "A good relationship will be mindful of a we/our outlook, not an I/mine outlook." Think about this statement.

We had one fellow who came in for counseling in one of our churches. He had married a darling girl, and he came in to talk. Landrum listened to him say, "I want to do this. . . . I want to do that. I am going to do this." Landrum asked, "What does your wife think of that?" He answered, "I don't know. I haven't discussed this with her." Landrum stated, "*You* don't have plans anymore. They now are 'our' plans, and you'd better go home and discuss these with her before you reach a conclusion." Not surprisingly, that marriage didn't make it. They are divorced at this moment. There was a basic flaw in their thinking—they had never made that transfer from one way of life to another.

Making a deliberate choice is a third similarity between converting and marrying. When you made your profession of faith, it was a conscious decision. No one made you invite Christ into your heart and life. When you married, nobody forced you either. We don't live in the day of arranged marriages. You may not have chosen to be female, but you chose to be married.

When I have gone off and made decisions without my husband, I have had to live with the result. Many times it is not pleasant. I happen to believe if you want to, you can talk your husband into anything that is good and right. If you can't, then go along with the next best thing for the sake of harmony, peace, and support. This cooperation can only help your union with your spouse.

Partnership

Let's move on now to the purposes of marriage and how we can uphold them. The Bible gives us three—partnership, pleasure, and parenting—so we'll start with the first. Marriage is a *partnership* with friendship as its basis. I trust you and your husband are good friends, and you enjoy being with him as much or more than with anyone else. Genesis 1:27 reads, "The Lord God said, it is not good for man to be alone, I will make a helper suited to his needs." There are lots of translations of that verse. Some say "helper suited to his needs," some "completer," "helpmeet," or "complement," but all have the same connotation. This is one who becomes a part of his life as a companion, a best friend. We are told the more two people have in common, the greater the chances are for a happy marriage.

God puts husbands and wives together. It is interesting that He knows who to join. We bring to marriage what the other needs. There are a lot of ways Landrum Leavell does not need me; there are ways in which I don't need him. We both have independent streaks, but in numerous ways we do need each other. We fit together. The longer you live together, the more you fit. You both truly become one. It is exciting, and you will find over the years that as you share with one another you will grow closer.

Humans feel a need to belong. We can ascertain this from the remarriage rate following divorce if from nothing else. Statistics show that four out of five men and three out of four women remarry within five years of divorce. What they are saying is, "I haven't given up on marriage, I have just given up on one partner." This also is seen in widows or widowers, who feel the need to be with someone, to enjoy companionship or partnership.

In my marriage, the greatest ego trip I can take is to tell myself Landrum Leavell is not complete without me. Isn't that neat? Not only that, but I'm not complete without him. That's neat, too. I think we need to understand we are essential. We provide in marriage what is needed by our spouses, and pondering one's worth to one's lover builds self-image.

So if marriage is supposed to put two people together in a partnership, how are decisions going to be made? Any group of two or more people needs the principle of leadership. God knew that. You are familiar with the Ephesians passage that instructs, "Women are to be in subjection to their husbands, and men are to love their wives as Christ loved the Church." Landrum always says, "You show me a woman who is loved like Christ loved the Church, and I will show you a woman who has no trouble submitting to her husband."

Another translation of that word "submit" is to place another person in the position of honor and respect. If you are married to one you cannot honor and respect, you are outside the will of God. God saw fit to put the man in the leadership capacity and we are to adapt our lives to him. Here is a good definition of biblical submission I read: "one equal willingly placing himself or herself under the authority of another equal." We are equals in Christ. My husband is not over me and I am not under him, although I have a friend who jokingly said, "Who wants to be equal when if you just use your good sense, you can remain superior!"

I can give you a testimony at this point because I had problems with submission. I am independent and I married a leader. Landrum was going to lead or die trying. Of course he understood God's plan and knew that was the role assigned him. I was not, at that time, a willing follower. For many years I went along kicking and screaming until through a study of God's Word, I saw for myself this was *His* plan. It changed my whole attitude, and I became more willing to follow my husband. At least I didn't dig my heels in *every* time he exerted strong leadership in our family!

It is not a question of who is more important in the partnership. Somebody said it is like trying to decide which sleeve of a shirt or which blade of a pair of scissors is more important. They are equally necessary. Leadership is more a matter of what roles are assigned to us. We need to understand a family is in deep trouble if the husband and father is not in a place of leadership. Every organization has a president, and God ordained him to be president. I want you to pray for your husband that he will be the leader he ought to be. You won't have any fear of putting your life voluntarily under him if you know he is being led by God. He will then be a fit leader for you and the other members of your family.

Maybe you are saying, "My husband won't lead." Through the years I have had women tell me this, and they have been some of the saddest people I know. I can remember one young girl who came to me and said, "Mrs. Leavell, I would love for my husband to take charge. I would give *anything* if he would lead. We have been married eleven years and he has changed jobs ten times." My heart went out to her.

If you find that you are the dominant member of your family, you must seek ways to encourage your husband's leadership. It is developed exactly like a muscle—by exercising it. Put decisions on him; lean on him.

Landrum has encouraged me in that way. I had never really made a decision before we married. I couldn't even pick out a dress by myself—I always shopped with my mother. I still don't make decisions very well, but Landrum insists I do it because practice is the only way to develop this area.

Teach your children to make decisions. I remember taking Roland to spend five dollars he received on his sixth birthday. I took him to a toy store for this *big* expenditure. Of course you know what kids do. He looked and looked. I thought he never was going to spend his money. I apologized to the saleslady for taking so much of her time, and will never forget her reply. She said, "This is the best training possible for him to learn to make decisions."

Thrust leadership on your husband, especially if it is not his inclination to develop in that area. Make sure you and your children get plenty of decision-making practice in too. This way everyone is active in the partnership and strengthens it. Our roles are different, and we are incomplete without the other.

Pleasure

Pleasure is a second purpose of marriage. My good friend Nancy Sullivan said, "It is impossible to be a good pastor's wife if you are not a good wife to the pastor." Ruth Graham advised, "It is not our business to convert our husbands, we are only to love them." Mrs. Norman Vincent Peale declared, "I have only one project and he is my husband." Serving God includes serving your husband. We need to underscore that fact. The pleasure of sexual intimacy is one facet of the marriage relationship and one that grows out of love and keeps a marriage strong. We join our lives to the life of another in a one-flesh relationship, which God called "very good." Let's look at sexual pleasure between spouses, and then the issue of extramarital affairs.

I needed a lot of adjustment in the area of marital relations also. I grew up in a home where sex was never mentioned. As far as my mother and I have ever discussed, I have four children and I don't know how they got here! As a result, talking about this subject is not easy for me even now.

When I first started teaching Bible studies on the Christian home, Landrum asked me if I ever dealt with the sex relationship. I said, "Heavens, no!" His reply was, "You'd better! Of the couples who come to me for counseling, this is the problem 95 percent of the time. You had better deal with it."

So slowly but surely I have tried to talk about this problem area. I finally came to the conclusion that I didn't need to be ashamed to discuss what God was not ashamed to' create! He created this relationship. It still blows my mind, but this is biblical. You see, the Bible is very "pro sex." "Therefore shall a man leave his father and his mother, and shall cleave unto his wife: and they shall be [become] one flesh." Remember that this word "become" suggests a process.

Something else my husband told Ann at the counseling session before her marriage was, "You are not going to leave the wedding ceremony in perfect unity." Someone said, "Making love is an art to be worked on for years." Keep in mind that sex is God's gift and is the natural inclination for a husband and wife who love each other.

Sexual relations can cement a marriage, but they cannot solve all its problems. The difficulty is that we come to marriage from two different backgrounds. We stand before the minister dressed in the raw materials of our prior lives. Just as though you were going to build a house, you and your mate dump your pile of raw materials at the marriage altar. Then you both spend a lifetime putting them together.

My raw materials were my background, my family traditions, my poor self-image, and my attitude toward sex. In Landrum's pile were his background, his parents, his good self-image, and his attitude about so many things. We have spent all our married years putting the raw materials together. We have childhood scars, habits, and personalities that are very different.

Chances are, the way you observed Christmas was not the same. How you feel about many things will be widely divergent, and reconciling these differences is often a long, long process.

Sex was an area where my background was limited. I remember discussing the sex relationship in my Sunday School class one Sunday. I made the statement that for twenty-one years of my life, I was told, "No, no, no." Then with one thirty-minute ceremony it became, "Yes, yes, yes." I'm sorry, but I just don't shift gears that fast! When I made that statement, one of my class members responded, "Oh, Mrs. Leavell, that isn't what it should have been. It should have been, 'Wait, wait, wait,' then, 'Yes, yes, yes.'" Teach your children that concept. Marital intimacy is God's gift to the newlywed, but it is not to be opened early. God gave us the guidelines concerning His gift of sex.

The husband-wife relationship must be kept in good condition, because neglect inside the marriage often generates temptation outside of marriage. We can protect our husbands if we keep them sexually satisfied at home. There are one or two in every congregation only too glad to take advantage of a bad relationship and destroy a marriage and ministry. If you are a minister's wife, your greatest contribution to the Lord and His church may be to make a happy home for the preacher.

I agree with this statement: "Sexual breakdown is related to the general absence of marital intimacy. It is rarely physical, the plumbing nearly always works." I don't know about you, but I don't categorize my life. If I am mad at my husband, I can't go into the bedroom and pretend everything is wonderful. I've heard super sex is the climax of an attitude that has been set all day.

Sometimes we think men make sex number one on their list of

marital essentials. Statistics prove otherwise, ranking it about fourth. One survey said 74 percent of those questioned put companionship in first place. However, sex still is a vital part of marriage.

Perhaps it is not uppermost in our minds, but it becomes uppermost if it is not right. Let me illustrate. If you haven't eaten all day, you think about food. That doesn't mean eating is the most important thing in life, but it becomes that if you have been denied food for any reason. The same goes for sex. Paying attention to the importance of pleasure in your marriage can make it stronger.

Let's stop right here and talk about affairs. I don't talk about this very well, but I think somebody needs to say something about what is going on in our day. We have seen the Jim Bakkers and the Jimmy Swaggarts rise and fall. People are *wide-eyed* over this sort of thing going on among the clergy. What I resent to the very core of my being is the fact they have made *me* lose credibility. Anywhere I go now people say, "What do you think of Swaggart?" They are suggesting that since I'm in the ministry, I may cheat one day too. I think these clergymen have done all of us an injustice. Conducting extramarital affairs is *not* acceptable behavior.

We must learn from the mistakes of other people—we don't have time to make every mistake ourselves. Churches will put up with most anything but laziness and immorality. I agree with John MacArthur, who says preachers have only one shot at ministry. The same God that requires premarital chastity requires postmarital fidelity. Understand this fact.

The writer of Proverbs mentions two sexual abuses, adultery and fornication. It is generally believed adultery is sex outside of marriage and fornication is sex between singles, and both are wrong. The whole book of Proverbs spells out the risk and the high price you pay if you go against God's plan in either of these areas. The thing I have never understood is why some men think they are such Casanovas. Anybody who will run around with you while you are married, will run around with somebody else when married to you. Doesn't that make sense?

Consider this statement: "A great lover is someone who can satisfy one woman all her life long and be satisfied by one woman all his life long. A great lover is not someone who goes from woman to woman to woman." The real man is one who can satisfy one woman for fifty years rather than one night.

I feel that same way about a pastor's responsibility. It takes a lot more study, work, ingenuity, and creativity to get up a sermon every week and satisfy a congregation over the long haul than it does to preach every week in a different church and preach the same set of sermons. When God calls us, He intends for us to do a good job, whether in marriage or church. We must keep both in a constant state of repair.

We hear a lot today about forgiveness. People ask if I will forgive Jimmy Swaggart, and the Bakkers. I don't have to forgive them. If God has forgiven them, that is good enough for me. However, when we emphasize only forgiveness we are emphasizing just one aspect of the Gospel. What about purity, leadership, and repentance? These other things are just as much a part of the Gospel. Mark it down—*the position of leadership brings with it some discretionary codes of conduct.*

This is not only true for your husband, it is true for you as well. Proverbs refers to the foolish and the wise. The foolish are those who engage in adultery and fornication. Nelson Price holds that there are at least sixteen people injured in every affair. The number would be even higher for television personalities or other prominent people. As wives, we must decide to be faithful. Faithfulness is a mind-set. You don't wait until you are faced with the opportunity to decide whether or not you are going to be faithful. I hope every woman reading this has already decided to be faithful "till death do us part."

They say that within an hour, if you wanted to be unfaithful sexually, you could have the opportunity. If you want to be a loose woman, opportunities abound. We determine ahead of time whether we are going to be faithful or unfaithful. Unfaithfulness is never an option for the Christian.

If you are to remain faithful, you must guard your "thought life." Jimmy Swaggart, for one, obviously let his thought life get away from him. My pastor said in a sermon, "If you don't nip something in the bud in your thought life, it will become an act. An act becomes a habit, a habit character, and character becomes destiny." Do you see the progression? It begins with thoughts. You have got to monitor your mind. Don't let your imagination run away with you, but put those impure thoughts out of your mind before injuring those you love. Lust is sin and will always lead to disobedience of God's will. Believing you are immune to immorality is naive, because it can happen. Just think of David and Bathsheba.

In ministry there are accepted modes of conduct. You must protect yourself and your husband from the appearance of evil. It may be necessary to accompany your husband on pastoral visits occasionally to avoid any possible criticism. Encourage him to do the little things that are so important, like never going behind closed doors for counseling with the opposite sex, especially after hours when the offices are empty.

Landrum tells this to his class on evangelism every year: "If my W.M.U. president was walking down the street in the rain, and I was driving by alone, I would not pick her up." They look at him in amazement. He had the advantage of being raised in a Baptist preacher's home where he was warned about such things. Most of us have not had that sort of background and training, but you cannot be too careful.

In this day some preachers think nothing of taking the secretary to lunch unaccompanied. This is unacceptable conduct for those concerned for their witness *and* the reputation of ministers. You need to watch the close relationships that develop because of ministry.

Even the most meticulous can be the victim of criticism coming from an emotionally disturbed person. When all else fails, *run*. Isn't that what Joseph did in the Scripture? Leave your coat if you have to, but get out. There are a lot of people who take delight in starting rumors, so wisdom dictates avoiding any possible compromising situation. "He who would lead the orchestra *must* turn his back on the crowd" is a saying applicable here.

Someone said, "Loyalty is more than avoiding an affair, it is having an affair with your spouse." Illicit relationships often come when the marriage has gone unattended for an extended period of time. We are God's priceless gift to our marriage partner. He planned, brought us together, united us in this bond, and it is up to us to keep it in good repair. "We need to be a lady in the parlor, and a hussy in the bedroom, and never get the two mixed up," was one person's advice. Another said, "We need to have a little bit of Betty Crocker, a little bit of Mother Theresa, and quite a bit of Raquel Welch." Providing pleasure in marriage will solidify its bonds, and keep temptation at bay.

Making a Marriage Grow

Parenting, along with partnership and pleasure, is one of the biblical purposes of marriage, and I will discuss the parent-child relationship in the next chapter. As far as your relationship with your husband, however, it is important to keep it healthy and growing.

We have been looking at several ways so far to keep a marriage healthy: making a successful transition from life with parents to married life, forming a strong union with your husband, becoming partners, providing pleasure and preventing affairs. Assuming that these things are being taken care of, there are at least two other factors involved in making a marriage grow.

The first is encouragement. As I've said earlier, remember to promote, compliment, and praise your husband. Others do. He is in a highly visible position. He is going to get a lot of strokes and you certainly don't want him to get all of these from others. Affirm daily the attributes you cherish in him. Praise is an indirect form of romance. Fill him up with admiration and he will shower you with love. So often we are quick with our criticism, but just remember he needs to be loved, not changed.

We come to marriage with "I do" and then often start to "redo." As one person has put it, "A woman marries with the ridiculous idea that she can change him. A man marries with a naive idea that she will stay the same." A woman makes a much better wife when she does not try to make her husband better. She needs to start there— not trying to "redo," but just trying to love the one she has.

The other important factor in nourishing a marriage is court- ship. My family doctor always advised young couples to keep courting. The best way to keep your marriage in good shape is to rediscover romance and duplicate some of the circumstances you used to enjoy. One of the reasons for marital conflict is growing accustomed to having your mate around, or just plain boredom. Keep doing some of the little things, the surprising out-of-the-ordinary things, that lend excitement and joy to your marriage. If you don't, it will get stale and turn sour.

I read this suggestion: "For one month try doing the things that you would do if you were still trying to get your husband to propose." For some reason we don't keep doing that, do we?

Marge Caldwell suggests that we plan something to do together at least every two weeks. Take your children sometimes, but not always. A baby-sitter may be the best money you and your husband spend. Keep having a date night. Have *fun*. Everybody needs to escape job pressure, relax, and enjoy themselves occasionally. Marriage, like a garden, has to be cultivated. There is not a safe stage when a couple can let weeds take over. Make a commitment to continuous cultivation regardless of the response your efforts meet. There may be times in marriage when one partner has to bear more than his or her share of responsibility.

Face the fact that changes probably will come gradually. Remember these three truths:

1) You can't change anyone else.
2) The only person you can change is yourself.
3) The exciting thing is that others change in response to the change in you.

If we can succeed in only one thing, let it be this most precious of all human relationships—marriage. Otherwise you will *miss the blessing.*

CHAPTER 7

LOOK AROUND:
Parent-Child Relationship

THE THIRD PURPOSE OF MARRIAGE is parenting. I must confess at the outset that I will be speaking from a real bias. I am a satisfied customer, having loved my role as a mother and a grandmother. I even like being a mother-in-law!

I was born the last of five children. I was one of those change-of-life babies and grew up almost like an only child. I always wanted a lot of children. I do have a big family now, for all of them to have been born by Caesarean section. Today, four children make a *big* family. But I love all that entails.

In Psalm 127:3-5 we read:

> Lo, children are a heritage of the Lord: and the fruit of the womb is His reward. As arrows are in the hand of a mighty man; so are children of the youth. Happy is the man that hath his quiver full of them.

We hear a lot today about limiting the number of our children. I am so glad I had my four before I could start feeling guilty about them.

Several years ago we went to China, and the thing that distressed me most about the Chinese was their government-imposed limit of one child per family. There are stiff penalties if you have additional children. The state won't give you money to provide for them or their education. Because I value the family so much, this policy really disturbed me.

The Importance of Parenthood

One pastor's wife has remarked, "Homemaking has been my primary career, with mothering the chief emphasis." I could say ditto. In a sense, if I fail at parenting, I haven't got anything else to show for my years spent on this earth. It has been my chief role for many years. If I were a missionary, I would probably be classified as "Church and Home" because of my two primary loves—marriage and parenthood. I think it is a high calling to be a wife and mother.

There is a lot being written today about mothering, but it is usually slanted by a veiled put-down. I want to tell you it is the grandest thing you could ever do. I think it is more important than making speeches, writing books, or succeeding in business. If there were no children, if we did not care for those children, no future generations would grow up to make their contribution to the world. In fact, a friend's daughter-in-law once claimed her children were her only *eternal possessions.* We spend a lifetime accumulating things, but our children are the only eternal possessions we have. Motherhood is a demanding role, but a rewarding one.

Children are the most important natural resource a nation has to offer. I read somewhere, "It can be demonstrated from history that no society ever survived after the deterioration of its family life." That is a scary thought. If we, as dedicated homemakers, turn out decent children, stable citizens, and godly men and women, we will make a contribution far greater than just trying to advance our own status in this world.

I know that when you have your hands full with little ones, it is easy to lose sight of the fact that what you are doing has eternal consequences. You are, however, raising citizens of tomorrow. Don't forget, after God your *first* duty is to those in your household.

The home is God's design, not just a practical arrangement. Sometimes we lose sight of the spiritual part of parenting. The home is God's plan and the Scriptures, especially the Old Testament, give a very positive view of home and family, children, and grandchildren. In fact Proverbs 17:6 says, "Children's children are the crown of old men and the glory of children are their fathers." One translation says, "Grandchildren are the reward God gives, they are the crown of old men."

People who choose not to have children are going to be lonely old people. As we get older, our children and grandchildren mean more to us. When they are little, we are covered up with responsibilities, but as we get older, they are the joy of life.

The Problems of Parenthood

Parenthood has been a satisfying role for me, but it hasn't been problem-free. I heard of an interview with Ruth Graham where she was asked, "Mrs. Graham, have you and Dr. Graham ever had any problems with your children?" I thought she gave the best possible answer. She said, "Dr. Graham and I have five children. We have children, we have problems." A glance at headlines today will reinforce the fact that parenting is not trouble-free. Read any newspaper and you'll see all sorts of problems that face parents.

Being good parents is one of the hardest things to do. One person said, "It is easier to command a large staff of people across a desk than to communicate with one teenage son across the dining room table." I would agree. Parenting is no picnic.

I always think of the story Landrum tells of a woman who boarded a bus with ten children. She had a rather haggard look as she got each one situated. As she sat down, the man next to her asked, "Are all these your children or is this a picnic?" She scowled at him and said, "They are all mine, and it is *no* picnic." My four were no picnic either. However, the problems are not paramount. The paramount thing is, we are doing what the Lord called us to do. We are doing something for Him as we raise godly men and women of integrity and high morals.

Children are the gift of God. Blessed is the man whose quiver is full of these arrows. Your children are arrows you send out into the world. If I do my homework well with my four children, I have four arrows going out into the world to bless, influence, and become spiritual leaders. To me that is exciting. An arrow suggests something that has been launched toward a target. You don't just throw an arrow, but you put it in a bow and aim at a target. You aim your children in a certain direction.

Good children don't emerge by accident. The Scripture says, "A wise woman builds." It takes planning. It is by design we raise godly children and send them out into the world. Children are the fruit of careful cultivation.

It grieves me that many children are not being cultivated carefully. They are not even being taken care of physically, much less being taught the things of God. They are not being prayed for or loved. Motherhood is truly a partnership with God. We can't do it by ourselves. We must depend on *Him*. With His strength and our determination to do a good job of mothering, we can succeed in this all-important partnership.

Howard Hendricks reminds us, "No amount of personal or professional success will ever compensate for parental bungling." Someone else observed, "Any other successes bought at the cost of your home and family are strangely and surely tarnished." There are a lot of people who could stand in testimony of that fact. They did not give their home the emphasis it should have had and many homes are in trouble today.

We have only to study the Old Testament to see the number of otherwise intelligent and successful adults who were tragic failures as parents. In my daily devotionals, I've been reading about David and Bathsheba, Absalom, and all their family problems. Here was David, "a man after God's own heart," but a tragic failure as a parent. We can be successful in our chosen fields, but miserable failures as parents. Someone said, "We can have a million-dollar business and ten-cent kids." The reverse of that is also true. We may have ten-cent businesses, but we can bless the world with million-dollar kids.

Yet let me hasten to add, even when we give it our best, children are free moral agents. We can still fail. I often quote this statement: "If your family is a failure, your testimony is a failure." I don't state that to put anyone on a guilt trip, because I am as aware as you, there are godly people who did the very best they knew how with their children and had a child who chose an alternate life-style. I don't know anything with the potential for more heartbreak than a wayward child. You are going to have such parents in your church, who need a sympathetic ear.

I don't have all the answers, but I do know something of the turmoil a child can create. Let me use a situation from my own family to demonstrate some of the common problems of parenthood. It also shows that, whether or not your children turn out to be "good," you cannot blame yourself if you have tried your best.

Our daughter is now happily married to a Baptist preacher. However, when Ann was a teenager she was a ring-tailed tooter. I wouldn't go back with her from fourteen to sixteen years of age for all the cows in Texas. We had three boys and one girl, but she was more difficult than all three boys put together. When we would tell people we had three boys and a girl, they would always say, "Oh, poor Ann." I always replied, "Don't waste any sympathy on Ann. She drives us *all* crazy."

Most of our problems centered on one boy in her life. I believe if you can get girls through the first serious, or what they think is serious, love affair you have probably got it made. She had her eye on this boy who was seventeen, two years older than she was. We never believed such an age difference was healthy in high school, because older boys just know too much. I didn't want him to even come near my daughter, much less date her, so we didn't allow it. Ann rebelled but I am very grateful Landrum is such a strong daddy. Encourage your husband to be the leader. If I had not had a strong husband, I am *convinced* we would have lost Ann to someone unsuitable at the time.

Mothers usually are soft. Ann could have talked me into letting the bars down. She would say, "Oh, Momma, can't he just come over? We won't go anywhere." It would have been so easy to say yes. Landrum said, "No." All the tears she was capable of using didn't faze him. It *killed* me.

I remember one of the things she said that absolutely broke my heart. She told me, "Momma, the thing I don't understand about you and Daddy is you just don't believe people can change." If she had stuck a knife in me, it couldn't have hurt any worse. I replied, "Honey, our whole ministry is built on the fact that we believe people can change, and that God can change people. I want to tell you one thing. I am not going to find out if this boy has changed on my little girl!" Landrum and I held the line.

We didn't know what she was going to do. It got so bad we threatened to send her away to school. Landrum has always said you have to risk losing your children to save them. Remember that when you get to the tough places. It is worth the risk.

When we put those limits on her, we didn't know whether she was going to run away, or run off and then marry him. You don't know all those things, but you have to do what you feel is right as the Lord leads you. You cannot listen to your peers. My friends kept saying, "Oh, Jo Ann, you are just going to make her more rebellious. She is going to sneak off, she is going to do this and that." All that may be true. It probably was a high risk we took, but we did what we felt was right before the Lord.

I say all that to say this. Had Ann chosen an alternate life-style, had she kicked over all the traces and gone in another direction, the *only* way I could have kept my sanity was to feel I had done my best. I finally in tears before the Lord said, "Lord, I don't know what else I could have done." If I had it to do all over again, I don't know what I would have done differently.

Just imagine my guilt if I had been a lackadaisical parent, and Ann had chosen to go her own way. I don't see how I could have survived. You just do the very best you can. Keep your children in church and as close to the Lord as you possibly can. Let's look at three other ways you can help direct your children as you raise them. These are: showing an interest in them, teaching them integrity, and getting involved in their lives.

Interest

Seek to learn all you can about parenting. Often today's parents "are blamed and not trained." I want us to look at our responsibilities in the light of biblical teaching. Parenting is a long-term investment, according to the Bible. It is not a short-term loan, and it demands our best efforts.

The first thing I would suggest is *interest* in our children. This interest ought to be expressed in *love* and *limits*. I heard this at a PTA meeting one time: "Children need love and limits, then let them alone." That statement impressed me and I have remembered it all these years.

I have also heard, "Children are not things to be molded, they are people to be unfolded," and, "The home is a factory that makes people." All of our energy is going into making these little ones responsible people. This unfolding process takes place best in an atmosphere of love. Proverbs 15:17 says, "Better is dinner of herbs where love is, than a stalled ox and hatred therewith." In our parlance, better is hamburger with love than steak without it. Love is the ingredient we need to provide, and that goes for everyone in your family, not just the children.

They say the greatest thing you can do for your children is to love their father. Children need to *see* that love and affection around them. When Lan was a little boy about two and Landrum and I were hugging or kissing, he would come up, get between us, and say, "What is going on here?" If you are liberal with your affection to one another, your children will benefit. Your husband needs to be your top priority. Don't let him be like the man who remarked, "I haven't had a wife since our first child was born." Keep your husband in first place.

Next, love your children. They are the result of your love for your husband, and they need to be treated as loved objects. Marge Caldwell reminded us at a marriage enrichment weekend to love our children unconditionally. We shouldn't say to our children, "I love you because . . . ," or "I love you if . . . ," but "I love you *period*." This is the way our Heavenly Father loves us.

I can remember hearing a politician's wife speak at one of our ministers' wives luncheons at the Southern Baptist Convention. She had a "his, hers, and ours marriage." Both she and her husband had been married before and had children, then they had a child together. Between them they had eight children. She shared with us the problems she had with some of her stepchildren not accepting her in the home and as a mother. There was one particular little boy who gave her fits. He was determined she wasn't going to stay. He thought if he acted ugly enough he was going to run her off and then he would have his daddy back. She said she prayed and cried before the Lord over and over again about what she was going to do with all of these children, but especially the one dealing her such misery. She said she finally got peace about it and told the little boy, "I love you and I am here to stay. There is nothing you can do that is going to run me off." This is unconditional love.

Sometimes our children "try" us. I frequently offered mine for sale *cheap*, in jest. However, our exasperation with them is not to be interpreted as a lack of real love. Even the Holy Spirit can be grieved. We love them with the unconditional love we've learned from our Heavenly Father and nothing they can ever do will change that rock-solid certainty.

It's been observed that "a child has not benefited if his parents provide for his material needs, but overlook his need to be loved." There are many children starving for this kind of affection. Intellectually I knew my parents loved me, but I needed to "hear" it. Your children need to hear it. Hold them close in love. Kids have an innate desire to be loved and they must get that sort of affection at home. Otherwise, you are going to send them out looking for love experiences in strange places.

Be vocal in your expressions of love. Let them know you love them, and look for ways to show it. This is not just with children but all those under your roof. Look for ways to show affection and be specific: "I love you because . . ." and always mentioning character qualities rather than physical qualities. Don't let children suffer under pressure for perfectionism, but give them love and acceptance. The way they think later in life will be influenced to a great degree by the way we talked to them, treated them, and loved them.

There is a big difference between appreciation and affirmation. You appreciate people because of what they *do*. You appreciate your child when he or she cleans his room. You appreciate your children when they do positive things. However, affirmation is on the basis of what they *are*. Even if they fail at *doing* something, they can be affirmed. The technique is to affirm a child at a higher level than his present one. As they say, "Hold a crown a few inches above your child's head and then watch him grow into it." That technique works.

Showing an interest in our children also involves setting limits. Sometimes we think love and limits are mutually exclusive. Not so. We might just call this "tough love." That is what we showed Ann in those years when she was fifteen and sixteen. You'd better believe that was tough love, but rules without the relationship will equal rebellion. We gave her love and tried to set some limits. She was rebellious in spite of our efforts, but had there been no love, she would have been long gone. Don't try restrictions without affection or your efforts will be futile. It also works the other way. Really loving your children means setting some guidelines.

Someone said that house rules for children are like a pole beside a tall plant. The pole doesn't hinder the plant's growth, but helps guide it. When you discipline your children, this is what you are doing. You are providing a pole, a stake, so they don't bend and lean, but stay upright and grow in the correct direction. A network of strong roots develops, stabilizing growth.

Understand up front that being a parent is not a popularity contest. In fact, Landrum always relates that if he had been burning up, Ann would not have spit on him during those teenage years. I asked her one time, "Honey, why are you so mean to Daddy?" Then I answered my own question, "Is it because he is the final authority?" She nodded. He wasn't running in a popularity contest. He was setting limits, doing what he felt was right to do, whether she liked it or not.

Proverbs 19:18 (N.I.V.) says, "Discipline your [child], for in that there is hope; do not be a willing party to his death." In other words, discipline is necessary. Pruning is necessary for the plant to grow right.

Another thing Landrum always said was, "My children are not going to learn obedience from a fellow in a blue suit and badge. They are going to learn obedience at home." The home is where obedience needs to be taught, but the toughest thing to do is to be consistent and follow through.

I remember one time I told Landrum, "Be careful what you promise in the way of discipline but once promised, see it through." I made that statement because of what I had observed from friends who had a son about the age of one of our boys. Lan came in one day and announced, "Momma, Jim was supposed to be grounded for six weeks. It has only been two and he is already off." I saw Lan laugh because they were not sticking to their ground rules.

It is so easy in a moment of anger to say, "You are grounded for six weeks." Do you know how long six weeks can be? It can be an *eternity*. It is best to ground a child for shorter periods of time, but stick to what you say. Ecclesiastes 5:5 points out in the Living Bible, "It is far better not to say you'll do something than to say you will and then not do it." Don't forbid anything unless you stand by it. Consistency is hard, but it is the *key* to good discipline and is said to be the *one* common characteristic of those who impact our lives.

There is a difference between discipline and punishment. Discipline is "for" a child and looks to the future. Punishment is done "to" a child and looks to the past. A lot of our discipline can be preventive as we look to the future and do what is best for that child. However, punishment is called for when our attempts at preventive disciplining have failed.

An obedient child is made, not born. Proverbs 22:15 says, "Foolishness is bound in the heart of a child, but the rod of correction shall drive it far from him." Proverbs teaches us most of what we know about raising children. Look at 13:24: "He that spareth his rod, hateth his son: but he that loveth him chasteneth him betimes." Proverbs 29:15 states, "The rod and reproof give wisdom: but a child left to himself bringeth his mother to shame." Pay attention to these verses and understand that love and limits are part of our parental responsibility.

My little grandson once sat down to lunch and promptly said, "I don't like broccoli." I told him, "I didn't give you much—you are going to eat your broccoli." He refused. I tried to be calm. I said, "Andrew, you may sit there *all* afternoon, but you are going to eat your broccoli." He tried every way imaginable to get out of it. It would have been a lot easier for me to compromise, believe me. Laziness is often the reason we don't follow through with our discipline.

Children's happiness with our imposed boundaries is not the issue. Understand that children are going to challenge every limit. That is just born in them, but don't be deterred by their objections. I don't know any child who is happy with boundaries. I will add another tip: don't "see" everything. Someone said, "The art of being wise is the art of knowing what to overlook." You can't punish for everything a child does. Pick important things, those dangerous ones leading a child in the wrong direction.

"Provoke not your children to wrath" is a biblical admonition. We provoke and discourage them when we are too hard. Overlook those things that don't really matter but insist that punishment always follows a significant trespass.

Establish the boundaries well in advance. Let a child know what is expected, and it is a *must* for parents to discipline together. Children are artists at dividing their mothers and daddies. They go to you and say, "Momma, can I do it?" Then they go to Daddy and say, "Can I do it?" He usually says, "What did Mother say?" They will separate you poles apart if they can. This is why children can be a potential for crisis as well as a possibility for growth in marriage.

In the establishment of these boundaries, there must be a connection between the sinful behavior and painful consequences. A child must know there will be painful consequences if he disobeys. If Andrew had left the table without eating his lunch, I would have punished him. If I am going to keep my grandchildren, I am going to have the prerogative to administer the punishment necessary. It must follow disobedience, and not according to how mother or grandmother feels or if mother has a headache. If we state the boundaries, and then punish after disobedience, the child gets the message his conduct is not acceptable. He learns it is not too smart to disobey if he is going to have correction. A child learns to say "no" to himself only by being told "no" by parents. The goal is to teach self-discipline and self-control.

Yet there is no reason to be overly restrictive. You really should try to say "yes" as often as possible to your children's wants. Don't get in the "no" habit. I learned this the hard way from two little boys who had befriended my son David. They lived behind us. I can remember telling them to go ask their mother if they could eat lunch with us. "She will say yes," they answered. I would ask them to get her permission for various things, and they often responded, "She will say yes." My children would probably have said, "No, she won't let me." Say "yes" as often as you can, but when you do say "no," make it stick. By providing love and limits, you are showing an interest in your children's welfare.

Integrity

Integrity is the second necessity for effective parenting. Moral integrity is taught, not caught. "Children may close their ears to advice, but they open their eyes to example" was one person's observation. Someone else said, "So live that you wouldn't be ashamed to sell the family parrot to the town gossip." Parents are the most effective communicators of values *if* the standards they teach are the ones they practice.

Being an example is hard work. Children tend to copy you at your worst moment! And what you do in moderation, your children will do in excess.

With that statement, I can't help but think of the alcohol problem in our society today. Watch the children of social drinkers. What those parents do in moderation, their children often do in excess. I have seen it too many times.

Parents are not commanded to produce godly children, but to be godly parents. Someone said, "My father didn't tell me how to live— he lived and let me watch him do it." What a super statement. Really, the hard work that we put in our own maturity will be an investment in our children.

My husband heard a speaker make a statement which we think is accurate. "Children love their mothers but they *follow their daddies.*" That ought to be a sobering thought for any fathers out there. Men, beware of the high cost of low living! Psychologists claim a bad example produces a bad effect for five generations. That is downright *scary.*

One survey shows the average time fathers spend with their young sons per day is thirty-seven seconds. That is not enough time to exert a positive influence. If we want to be models for our children, we have to spend time around them.

Somewhere I read, "The frightening thing about heredity and environment is that parents provide both." The way to change our children is to change ourselves. If we are growing, our children are going to be growing. This is how it works.

Involvement

This leads me to say a word about *involvement.* Are you involved in the life of your child? It is your job to work with him daily and teach him how to make proper choices. You can't cram religion down his throat. You can't give "your" faith to him. It must be his faith, and he is most likely to find it for himself if you are deeply involved with him.

Deuteronomy 6:7 says, "Use every opportunity to teach your children about God and His commandments." If we don't teach them, they are going to be handicapped for life. There are many spiritually handicapped children like that around. So, without imposing ourselves too much on our children's lives, we need to get somewhat involved in their spiritual growth.

When you pot a plant, you don't actually *make* it grow, but you provide the required conditions—good soil, water, and sunshine. God provides the growth. It is the same way with children. We need to provide the conditions under which growth is most likely to take place.

One way to involve yourself with your children's lives is to pray for them. Begin when they are little and continually pray for them all the way up. If possible, take on the project of praying for somebody else's child too.

Don't only pray, but be present in your children's lives. They say, "Old-fashioned women can remember when a baby-sitter was called Mother." With the number of women now in the work force, I'm afraid that is changing. Children are in day-care centers and we are forfeiting our chance to be involved in their lives.

Landrum and I have paid our dues on the bleachers! All three of our boys were high school and college athletes. We made a conscious effort to be at every one of their games for support. I still have withdrawal every Friday night since my presence is no longer required at the stadium.

In Lan's senior year in high school, his football team went to the state finals. I remember well the day the semifinals were to be played in Amarillo. The weather was *terrible,* with warnings to stay off the snow-packed icy roads. Landrum asked, "What are you going to do?" I said, "I don't know about you, but I'm going!" This sort of involvement has paid rich dividends in happy memories.

I often wondered what a mother would do if her child happened to be the injured one in the pile-up on the football field. One afternoon when Roland was playing ball, I found out! My heart sank as I realized that was *my* child on the ground. Landrum didn't move until I asked, "Are you going down there or am I?" Roland probably would have added heart failure to his separated shoulder had I appeared on the field! I've always been glad we were present when he had a need for his parents.

David nearly caused us to forget our commitment of support the year he had a forty-two-game basketball schedule. The coaches played him on the junior varsity and varsity teams simultaneously. I had always prayed I would have the same enthusiasm with the fourth child I had with the first, hence my disappointment when Landrum announced one night he wasn't going to David's game. He said, "Honey, I know how you feel, but I'm tired, and there is a big difference in making every game of a football season and every game of *two* basketball schedules!" We needed the night at home, and I doubt David has held it against us.

One time when Ann needed some special attention we flew to Georgia for a week with relatives—just the two of us. What child wouldn't feel special to miss school with parental sanction? Another time we enrolled in a craft class together. It doesn't seem to matter what you do as long as you are deeply involved with your children in agreed-on activities.

When our children were small, one of our goals was an annual family vacation. We were campers in those days. This stemmed mostly from financial necessity, but allowed us to show our children much of this land of ours. Our trips have taken us from Canada to Mexico and from the Atlantic to the Pacific on limited funds. Much of our reminiscing today centers around these trips.

Parents should also become involved in PTA and other school functions. I think any child would relish having his or her mother serve as home-room sponsor. I've supplied hundreds of homemade chocolate chip cookies for such events.

In addition to all of this involvement, your presence never has more impact than when you worship together. Parents are constantly asking me, "How do you get a sixteen-year-old to church?" My answer is always the same. "You don't." The task will be extremely difficult unless you have led a two-year-old and four-year-old in regular habits of worship. Spiritual training needs an early beginning.

There is no substitute for your physical presence, especially when your children are little. As they get older, instant availability without continuous presence is probably the best role a mother can play. I always want to be instantly available for my children, even though they are married and have their own families. I make sure they know where I am and how to contact me at any time.

As children grow up, we are to give them supportive, loving withdrawal. "Mothers are not to lean on, but to make leaning unnecessary." We are really, in a sense, working ourselves out of a job, but never a relationship. We sow early in their lives through instruction, but reap later through friendship.

My family can tell you I am *big* on "togetherness." I like nothing better than to have my family together for *any* reason. Landrum still kids me about how many "last" trips we have taken. You know the line: "Honey, this may be the last time we can go anywhere together as a family!" We have made it a practice to go on trips together, attend functions where any family member was participating, and support with our presence any significant event. Interest in graduations, birthdays, weddings—even funerals—reinforces family closeness.

We all gathered recently in Jackson, Mississippi, for Roland's ordination as a deacon in First Baptist Church. I've never been prouder of my family as they made detailed arrangements to be away from pulpits, jobs, and other engagements to be there. I told Roland if they had awarded people for attracting the most guests to the ceremony, he would have won. This involvement in your children's lives is the key to family cohesiveness.

Parenting is a *wonderful* calling, an incredibly beautiful task. I hope you will show interest in your children—love them, and limit them when they need to be limited. Teach them integrity through your examples, and involve yourselves in their lives. And when you get to the stage where I am, you will say, "Lord, I did the very best I could." I promise you will never, never regret it. *Don't miss the blessing.*

CHAPTER 8

LOOK AROUND:
Communication

WE HAVE JUST BEEN LOOKING at some of the important relationships in our lives—with our husbands and our children. Communication, or lack of it, is always involved in such relationships, so now let's give it some careful attention. I will begin with communication in marriage, and then offer a few tips for promoting understanding within the family as a whole.

Landrum often reminds young couples they are not going to have a perfect marriage. They look at him in amazement. Somehow they think marriage means a perfect union. He tells them, "You can't put two imperfect people together and produce a perfect marriage."

According to Dr. David Mace, there are three essentials for a successful marriage. These are:

1) commitment to continuous on-going growth
2) *development of an effective communication system*
3) and ability to use conflict creatively.

God's plan is that two married people become one flesh, sharing their most intimate thoughts and experiences. If intimate partnership is God's purpose, how do we develop this "language of married love"? Communication is the bottom line in the "care and feeding of a happy marriage."

Angel Martinez spells love *t-i-m-e*. One of the most often repeated complaints I hear from couples is, "We don't have any time together." This is something *you* can correct. We hear a lot today about time management, and I'll go into this in the next chapter. You can't manage time, but you *can* manage the activities that fill your time. Get rid of the commitments that are eating into your time together. It's the little jobs that nibble away at the fabric of marriage and family life. I find this a provocative question: "What kind of a God would create persons male and female, place love in their hearts, call them to matrimony, and then begrudge them the time to keep love alive and growing?"

I'm told you need at least two hours a week to work on your relationship with your spouse. Schedule time alone with your husband just as carefully as you do exercise, worship, and any other appointments you value. Set aside special "ritual time" to spend with the one you love. Stay close to each other, so you can't use the children to camouflage estrangement. Good marriages have one thing in common—good communication, and good communication requires priority planning.

I will confess I was a pouter growing up. Have you ever pulled that on someone? I can remember not speaking to my roommate for three days when I was in college. I was the last of five children, very much the baby, and spoiled. I learned I could get what I wanted by pouting. I brought that bad technique into marriage. I tried it on my husband *once*. I never will forget it. I pouted. He looked at me with that look you've all gotten from your husbands, and he said, "Sit down." Then he said, "I just want to tell you something. We talked things out at my house, we didn't pout. Now say what you have to say."

I had to learn to communicate effectively. Do you need help? None of us ever arrive at perfection, but communication is the bridge between husband and wife. If the bridge is not down and operating, it becomes a wall between you.

It not only is important in the home but in every other avenue of life:

> 85% of our income is dependent on our communication skills.
> 71% of leadership is communication.
> 30% of our day is spent in talking, and 45% in listening.

It behooves us to improve our skills with this conversational tennis.

Before you say you don't need this discussion about communication, let me remind you that lack of communication is a problem to some degree in *every* marriage. It has been rated as the number one marital trouble. I don't think any of us communicate as well as we would like to, but keep in mind this is a *learned* skill with an extraordinary capacity to change lives. It is something we can do with just a little bit of encouragement and effort.

Often we think it is only the unsaved who have problems. I have a good friend who is a dedicated Christian. She says she has been married for more than twenty-five years, but has been only communicating with her husband for about four. She admits, "We did not talk or communicate, we did not really know each other at the deepest level. Now it is great. He tells me things he would never have told me a few years ago." Communication is the key to growth in a relationship, and it can be learned.

When you are dating, you can't talk enough. I can see this when I'm people watching at places like airports, malls, and restaurants. If the couples are talking, most of them aren't married.

My elderly mother pointed this out to me while visiting once. We were sitting on my front porch; the administration building was then right across the street. At five o'clock there is a mass exodus of secretaries as they head home. Mother was not a big talker, but she commented on a couple who came out. She said, "They must not be married." I asked her why she would make that statement. She answered, "Look at them—he has his arm around her."

Pick out couples who are really looking at each other. If they are listening to each other and enjoying the company of one another, they are probably dating. Marriage somehow shuts down conversation. Frequently with the marriage ceremony, we go from our man's number-one admirer and confidante to his number-one critic. We need to improve the way we communicate. Let's look at the different ways.

Five Levels of Communication

We blame a communication block on a lot of things. We blame it on the kids. We blame it on the fact that our husbands are never home. Laying blame won't cure the problem. Let's not live at this superficial level.

I'm told there are five levels of communication. Determine where you fit in. The first is called the cliche level. Talk sounds like: "How did you sleep?" "How was work today?" "What do you think the weather is going to do?" There is nothing threatening about any of these statements.

The next level is reporting facts about others. It sounds like the five o'clock news. "Did you know so and so was pregnant?" "Did you know so and so is being transferred?" "Did you hear he got another church?" If that sounded like your breakfast conversation this morning, you should consider leaving discussions of people and the weather to anchor people on television.

The third level of communication is when you begin to express your ideas or opinions, but if you run into any negative response or "put-down," you are prone to stop. Husbands and wives need to express themselves. Most of us are not willing to open up, even to our spouses. Our poor self-image often causes us to withhold our opinions, ideas, and personal feelings even from our loved ones. If you are at this third level of communication, begin to trust your husband with your feelings. If he is receptive, then you can give him more.

We should be trustworthy also. Our husbands must be able to confide in us with no fear of betrayal or ridicule. We must not criticize "stupid answers" or "wrong conclusions." Resist the temptation to be judgmental. Remove "never" and "always" from your vocabulary. After all, if he can't tell you, whom can he tell?

The fourth level is expressing your feelings openly. Tell your husband how you feel about any- and everything. Tell him how you feel about the children, your sex life, or your lack of companionship. Use "I" statements, not "you" statements. Tell him your feelings, *not* his faults!

Do you know what will happen if you bottle up negative feelings over a period of time? Eventually it will be like a singing tea kettle. The top is going to blow off. Then you are going to have *real* problems. People walk out, do and say things they would never do under normal circumstances. Don't bottle up your feelings— express them. Remove "nothing is wrong" from your vocabulary.

The advice I give to the students in my seminary class is, "Tell him how you feel, but don't tell him what to do about it." Then the ball is in his court.

Talk about the things that are close to you, and about your fears. If not, you build up what someone has called the "resentment syndrome." You accumulate grievances and often these resentments come out in unpleasant ways, sometimes even in illnesses. You begin to throw out to your husband things that happened six months or six years ago which were never expressed. Isn't it better to talk about those things? Let him know how you feel. Agree that six-month-old complaints are not permissible.

Of course, the fifth level of communication is total transparency. I wonder if any of us will ever achieve that. A higher level of communication is a goal toward which we work.

Where are you in this business of communication? Reflect on your marriage and family situation. On a scale of one to ten, how would you rate your communication skills? They say there is nothing as easy as talking and nothing as difficult as communicating. Are you still at the cliche level, talking about trivial things? Are you at the second level, reporting facts about other people? Have you begun to express your feelings? This is good. Continue to express them. Open up some of these lines of communication that have been closed for so long, for until you and your husband are sharing at every single level, you are not true partners.

Improving Communication in Your Life

Here are several tips that can help elevate you into a higher level of communication. Your marriage can certainly benefit from these ideas, but so can your other relationships. The first important thing to be aware of is how to send positive nonverbal messages.

Remember that communication is far more than just an exchange of words. There is a silent language that accompanies conversation. We call it "body language." In fact, only 5 percent, or some say 7 percent, of our communication is verbal. Approximately 38 percent is vocal—the way you say things—and 55 percent is facial. Think about that. The way we say things can leave an entirely different impression. What about the sighs we give which speak volumes? You can raise one eyebrow and flare your nostrils and tell the whole world it stinks! You can salve your conscience by claiming you didn't say anything, but it sure left an ugly impression. If you want to communicate with others, try to be positive in your tone and facial expressions.

Hugging is the best form of nonverbal communication. Touching is therapeutic. It is believed in some quarters that there is healing power in the human hand to allay illness and anxiety. The Bible speaks of the "laying on of hands." Are you a toucher? The most direct means of communication and reassurance is touching. We say to our children, "Don't touch. Don't touch yourself. Don't touch him. Don't let him touch you." As a result of that, we are not touchers anymore. We don't give people a pat, or hug them, or show any affection. We are the real losers.

The meaningful touch is called "the silent language of love." It is the first way babies know they are loved. It often expresses what can't be put in words. The average person needs four hugs a day for survival, eight for maintenance, and twelve for growth. These forms of nonverbal communication can be helpful in your relationships.

As far as verbal communication goes, though, there are three major guidelines: plan it properly, speak lovingly, and listen actively. Good judgment should be used in planning your important discussions. Have a clear purpose in mind, making sure you will be attacking the problem and not the person. Pray before any discussion or confrontation. In the case of marital problems, talk to the Lord about it *before* you talk to your husband. Often I have talked to the Lord and then thought better of talking to Landrum. Maybe all we need to do is take it to the Lord and leave it, and get it out of our hearts. However, if we have prayed about it and get a green light from the Lord, then pick the time to talk to your mate.

The key to effective communication is planning a time and place without distractions. *Never* bring up problems after ten o'clock! Aren't things worse at night? For one thing, nobody sleeps after that, and then you are *shot* the next day. That is not the time.

Perhaps the discussion needs to be away from the scene of the problem. If it is over one of the children, you certainly don't need to try to communicate with all the little hands and feet around. You are going to need to set up a time.

These planned discussion times don't always have to center on a problem. You need to make way for casual conversation with your husband too. What about planning a date night? I tell my class that one of my favorite moments is when Landrum and I go to walk at night. We live on campus in New Orleans and have a marvelous place to walk. If we are at home, Landrum is either reading, watching the news, or dozing in his recliner. As we walk he usually asks, "Did I tell you what happened today?" It's a perfect time for communication. Take "we" time whenever you can find it.

The next guideline to better communication with people is to "speak the truth in love." If someone thinks that talking to you is a pleasant experience, you will be amazed how the channels of communication will open. *How* we say things is extremely important. We need to speak lovingly in our communication with all people. Much of our attention we lavish on our husbands, if we are fortunate enough to have one. Those who do not have husbands can lavish that same love and affection on others. If our churches are truly church "families," there are many family members who need our attention. Children who do not have mothers or daddies need surrogate parents. You could be that father figure or mother figure. There are people all around who need the love, attention, care, and communication you can give them.

I never will forget my daughter's second grade teacher. She was one of those dedicated, *great* teachers. She was precious. It was just after we had moved to Wichita Falls, and Ann really needed some attention. Mrs. Nealy provided that encouragement. I remember well the day she shared with me a little bit about her background. I asked her how many children she had. She replied she had one married daughter. She said, "I wanted six children, but the Lord didn't see fit to give me but one." She gestured toward her group of thirty second-graders and said, "If I had had six, I never would have had all of these." I thought, what a remarkable woman!

We may not have the families we wish we had. We may not have children, and don't understand why the Lord hasn't given them to us. Just remember there are those around you with your same need of encouragement and love. Let's communicate our love. Let's take the time to do it. Let's break down barriers, and talk about things that are close to us.

Listening actively is one of the most important guidelines of all.

Talk together. Communication is dialogue. It is not when we do all the talking, having our "say" and telling the other off. It is talking together *and* listening. Active listening is an important part of conversation. The principle is: "If you listen to me, I am psychologically bound to listen to you."

I have a niece who at one time was having marriage problems. I gave her a tape on communication which pressed home this need for dialogue. She confessed, "I always told him what I thought, then I would go off in the next room and nurse my wounds."

Nobody seems to have time to listen anymore. Some of our hesitance at this point may be fear. If we listen, some involvement may be necessary. Listen and see if you can "hear" the deepest needs of your mate. Listen with your mind and heart. Listen between the lines. Hearing the spoken word is easy, but actively listening for the real message requires more effort. You must look into people, as well as at them.

My same friend, who had been married more than twenty-five years, communicating only four, said if she is cooking something on the stove now and her husband comes in the kitchen to talk, she turns off whatever is cooking and gives him her undivided attention. It requires effort to listen attentively, and listening with our eyes helps.

A humbling statistic for those of us trying to communicate stated that "50% of your audience's attention may wander in the first five minutes of your talk." A part of the problem is the fact that we don't speak as rapidly as we listen. Studies show we speak around 125 words a minute, but we can hear 400 to 500 words a minute. As a result, we engage in mental side trips during sermons and speeches. We make a grocery list for Sunday dinner or plan our Monday activities, and when we stay gone too long, we miss the entire message.

This same thing happens in conversation. My daughter is perceptive and knows when I'm not listening. When she was little, she would hold my face between her hands as she talked. I always felt guilty on those occasions. "Children learn when they listen, but they won't listen unless they feel they are also heard" is a quote I read that shamed me. We must "listen" to our husbands and our children.

They will be encouraged to talk by our obvious willingness to listen, and two-thirds of communication should be that listening process.

In addition to the guidelines above, try these suggestions for improving communication in your family. Laugh and play together. Make time for those minivacations. One of our seminary students said to me, "Mrs. Leavell, we don't have any money to take a vacation, but I have decided we are going to have some minivacations. We are going to take an afternoon off one day a week." I thought, "Honey, you are going to make it." That was an indication she knew the value of sharing fun times.

Work together on various tasks. One of my greatest joys is working with my husband at the seminary. We work together almost like a "ma and pa business." When you work together, whether it is building a patio, doing yard work, or repairing something, that time is never wasted. The key is that you are doing it together.

Then of course, pray together. We decided when we married that we would pray together every night before we went to bed. Of all the things that will keep the bridge of communication open, this is the most important. It is the best insurance I know against building up resentment. *Every* family will experience hardships and disagreements. You must work out the day's problems in order to pray together that night. The Bible says, "Don't let the sun go down on your wrath."

The Three-Point Plan

Give communication some thought. I'm going to outline three things to remember as you strive for that high level of openness in your family.

I. *Stay in touch* —
Don't let physical distance come between you. If you live close to one another, schedule frequent visits. If not, use phone calls, letters, tapes, or any other creative way to stay in touch. Our families have resorted to a round robin on occasion to keep the widely scattered members posted. This could become a much loved "family tradition" for you too.

Here's how to do it. Write a good, newsy letter recounting recent events addressed to the family as a whole. Include the order in which the "robin" is to be sent, putting your name last, and mail it to the next person on the list. Ask him or her to add a similar letter of his or her own as soon as possible, and continue it throughout the family. When it returns to you, remove your old letter, write a new one, and start the robin on another round.

The rules are:

> Keep it moving. Do not delay more than three days if possible.
> Use the proper amount of postage.
> Save your old letters as a diary.
> One page per family is sufficient.

There are lots of other imaginative ways to stay in touch. One grandmother I read about chooses a book and records it on a tape, ringing a bell each time the page should be turned. She sends the book and tape at the same time, thus having a private story hour with her grandchild.

Landrum and I have always felt that phone calls are our family's best investment. Ann started her freshman year at Baylor soon after we moved to New Orleans. I remember that during the first couple of weeks she called home *every* afternoon about three o'clock. When Landrum came in, I would tell him about Ann's call. Finally he said, "Tell her not to call anymore." I replied, "No, I'm not going to tell her she can't call home!" He said, "Well, at least tell her to wait until after six o'clock." I said, "No, I'm not going to do that either." Obviously she was homesick and that was her lowest point of the day.

Lan's call always came on Sunday nights after church. Maybe that was the time which reminded him the most of home and family. Money was tight, so after a reasonable length of time we would try to wind the call down. I always knew that when Lan asked, "What else is happening?", it was obvious *his* need for conversation had not been fully met.

Even with calls, don't neglect to write letters. I'll never forget how important mail call was at camp or the thrill of seeing mail in my box during college days. Write down words and thoughts for your children they will treasure for a lifetime.

II. *Stay sensitive to need —*

I recall a friend of mine called me soon after two of our children moved from New Orleans. She said, "How are Roland and Lisa doing in Jackson?" I replied, "Fine." Then she paused, and said, "How are *you?*" A warm feeling swept over me as I was aware of her sensitivity to my need. Only another mother could know the emptiness and ache I felt.

We all have a need to be understood and appreciated. Communication comes easy with those who accept and love us. Needless to say, Beverly O'Reagan had my ear, and had I needed "to talk" it would have been easy to confide in her. Why? She knew my need and expressed it.

I'll always remember when David, our youngest son, asked me for some time at our next family get-together. I had no idea what he had in mind, but I honored his request. He went around the room and told us individually of his love and the specific prayers he had prayed for each of us. All were on target, and I'll never forget mine. He had asked the Lord to give me new and fulfilling projects for my "empty nest" years. It made me aware he was sensitive to my needs, and I might add, that prayer has truly been answered.

We all left that gathering feeling unparalleled warmth and affection for each other. It had resulted from one family member's willingness to be transparent. David's contention and mine is we must know more about each other than food preferences and pet peeves. Family closeness comes through interest in one another as we reveal our hopes, dreams, and fears.

Don't be afraid to show your children that you have needs. It is worth the risk. I didn't realize how little of this Landrum and I had done until after Ann married. She would call me about some problem she and Finis were dealing with. In an effort to encourage her, I usually responded with a similar situation we had encountered. She always answered, "I didn't know that—you never told us." In our desire to protect our children, we don't prepare them for the real world. And we make it difficult for them to be sensitive to our needs.

III. *Share your faith* —

Why are we so slow to talk about spiritual things, even with family? We can give children a head start in life if they grow up comfortable with talk about values, morals, and faith. Take advantage of those "teachable moments." Talk about how God is working in your life, obvious answers to prayer, and unexpected evidences of God's care. Help your children see that God is alive and well, and it will help them maintain their faith in this faithless generation. To combat the negative, provide a constant source of security.

We are such forgetful creatures, it is easy to lose sight of our heritage. Moses warned the people of his day that the time would come when they would forget the marvelous works God had performed on their behalf. Mothers can insure remembrance by sharing continually, day in and day out. There is no greater joy than to see our faith multiplied in the lives of our children.

Change is never easy. You may not see instant results from this three-point plan or the other tips listed earlier. But if you don't quit and lovingly persist, I'm confident you will see your family rise to a higher level of communication.

Let me leave you with this quote I found:

> When you stop talking, you stop trying—
> When you stop trying, you start dying.

CHAPTER 9

LOOK AROUND:
Time Management

TIME MANAGEMENT IS A fascinating subject for me. My interest in it began when I learned the "troublemakers" in marriage. Whenever Landrum and I generated discussions in marriage enrichment conferences or seminary classes on the special problems of marriage, time was a problem area that surfaced repeatedly. It appears to be a problem for everybody.

Another reason for my interest is that Christian author and speaker James Dobson affirms the two leading causes of depression in marriage are (1) low self-esteem and (2) fatigue and time pressure. These two critical matters work together, because every obligation we shirk is a source of guilt. When there are more commitments than we can possibly handle, self-esteem is further damaged by each failure.

The secular world's interest in the subject of time management also intrigues me. Many of you recently have been to some sort of training session for your job. You've attended a retreat, time management seminar, or conference to enthuse and encourage you to do a better job at your place of employment. The secular world puts emphasis on getting your life under control.

All of us feel time pressure. Certain people act as if they are the only ones with this problem, but everybody I know is in the same boat. Someone observed, "It is like a thousand open doors facing us, and we have to decide which ones to walk through." Innumerable causes are out there everywhere clamoring for our attention, and we've got to decide what's important, where we are going to spend

135

our time, and how to live. A vague "I want to put God first" attitude is not enough.

Have you ever wished for more than twenty-four hours a day? Surely you have. When I come to the end of a day, I often long for one or two more hours to finish all I have set out for myself. You have one hundred sixty-eight hours a week. That's it. You can't add to it; you can't subtract from it. You do, however, have a choice on how to spend it.

Alan Lakein, a time management expert, suggests that people don't lack time. One hundred sixty-eight hours is plenty of time to do everything we want to do. I more nearly agree with my husband, who says, "There's plenty of time to do everything *God* wants us to do." There's a difference. Often we confuse activity with achievement. Our very busyness may indicate shallowness. My job is to determine God's will as opposed to mine. That way, I'm going to have enough time to do God's bidding.

In Philippians 4:19 the Scripture says, "My God shall supply all your needs. . . ." Right there in black and white He's promised to supply our needs, and this includes time. Lakein says, "When we're pressured by time, it means one of two things:

1) either we're doing the wrong things or
2) we are doing the right things in the wrong way."

I would hope that we are not doing a whole lot of wrong things. I'm not discounting that possibility. We may be, and we need to work that out, but I feel most of us are probably doing the right things the wrong way.

I'm told people waste 80 percent of their time. That blows me away! It's incredible the way we squander our lives, and wasted time is the most extravagant and costly of all expenditures. Let's take a look at some of the consequences of poor time management, and then examine the three remedies: plan, prioritize, and produce.

Unseized Time

In his book, *Ordering Your Private World,* Gordon Macdonald gives us four laws about unseized time. That's exactly what wasted time is. The first law is, "unseized time flows toward my weakness." The besetting weakness could be watching too much television, talking on the phone, reading unworthy books, or just puttering. One of my weaknesses is procrastination. I heard somewhere a list of twelve ways to determine if you are a proscrastinator, and I qualified on all twelve!

The distressing thing about children is, they can have weaknesses just as their parents do. My son David loves people. He loves visiting with folks in the cafeteria at the seminary. He enjoys hanging out on the corner and talking with everyone who passes by. That's unseized time flowing toward his weakness. The only remedy is to exert some discipline and get back to the areas that need attention.

Macdonald's second law is, "unseized time comes under the influence of dominant people in my world." If you haven't set up your own time budget, then these dominant people come along and force their agenda and priorities on you. This is what happens to many ministers' wives. They don't have their own time blocked out, and strong personalities in the church come along to impose their expectations on them. They tolerate it, and then the first thing you know they're bogged down and fighting for dear life. Roles that are not thought through are the ones that can bury you.

I detest the idea that if you are in ministry, or in any other profession, you are not in charge of your time. A woman needs to budget her time no matter what her position. In fact I read that "women must balance their time more than men because they don't have wives!"

The only people you need to consult about your activities are the Lord and your husband, in that order. Ask yourself, does the Lord want me to do it? Does my husband want me to do it? Is this going to affect our family life adversely? Also, be careful how you pose the question to your husband. If you say, "Honey, you don't really want me to do this, do you?" you have worded it so he will advise you not to do it. Then you can smile and say, "My husband really does not want me to accept that duty." I have done this myself, and it sounds so spiritual—so submissive. But if the task is something you're confident the Lord wants you to do, then you can convince your husband instead of hoping he'll exempt you! My sister-in-law says, "Certainly I'm submissive to Bobby—anything I can't talk him out of I go along with."

When I first started teaching seminary wives, I asked Landrum the question (just like I've described), "Honey, you don't think I ought to teach this class, do you?" He said, "I believe I would." That wasn't exactly what I had in mind. Then I painted the darkest picture. "Okay, when I walk out every Tuesday night, and the dishes aren't done, and David has homework, and the house is in disarray, are you going to look pitiful?" He responded, "I probably will, but go ahead!" Needless to say, he has never said one word when I walk out on class nights.

What had I done by asking him? I made him a partner and enlisted his support! I tell my students at the seminary, "Don't take on any job without first talking with your husband. Otherwise you're asking for trouble. Sit down and discuss it. It is smart to enlist the help of one another."

Don't be captivated by dominant people in your church. Assume responsibility based only on what you feel is God's will and your giftedness, and how it will affect your family life. When you take control there is no one to blame but yourself when squeezed by time.

The third rule is, "unseized time surrenders to the demand of all emergencies." We're governed by what someone has called "the tyranny of the urgent"—events that cry out for immediate attention. Many times we have to run to the aid of a baby who cries out, but not all emergencies are like that. Not everything that cries loudest is the most urgent. Manual tasks scream more loudly for attention than mental or spiritual ones. In fact, the important activities, like Bible study, prayer, or a visit to a neighbor, do not cry out and demand attention. These patiently wait for us to realize their significance.

In a seminar at Lake Yale, Florida, Landrum heard a pastor say something he has never forgotten. He stated if he was going to church for visitation and got a call that the chairman of his deacons was at the hospital and may not live, he would go on to visitation. After visiting he would go to the hospital and check on the deacon. He said, "I know where that deacon's going if he dies, but I don't know where those that I'm going to visit will go if they die." He had worked out his priorities ahead of time.

The last law is, "unseized time gets invested in things that gain public acclamation." I don't suppose there's one of us who does not like praise. All of us like "strokes," but we can't live our lives on "strokes." We must do some things, whether or not they get praise, if they are right to do. Remember we do right because it is right, then it feels right. We must decide what's important and give this our full attention, whether it gets praise or not.

David doubtless has a lot more fun and gets more strokes in the cafeteria than he does studying Hebrew, but what will tell the tale in the long run? It's going to be Hebrew! That's what he's being graded on. We must invest our time in things that may not always gain the most attention, but that are right.

Determine how you waste time. Write down your activities for several days and obvious time-leaks will probably surface. We've got two choices: we can control our time or we can continue to *react* rather than *act*, wasting our most valuable commodity. In my judgment three things are required for us to invest our time. First we must plan!

Plan

If we don't plan, others will plan for us. It is just that simple. We *do* have control. We have the ability to guide and direct our lives, and planning ahead is the key, along with *writing it down!*

A lady came up to me after I had given a talk on "list making" and told me, "Mrs. Leavell, I am too busy to take the time to make a list." Isn't it funny those extremely busy people are never too occupied to tell you how busy they are? She could have made her list in the length of time it took her to take me aside for her remark. Merely talking about the time you lack *is* a waste of time.

Get a calendar and mark it. Writing down your plans is the key. For one thing, it takes away the pressure to remember. They say memory is the first to go! I don't know about you, but if I don't write my "to do's" down, I can easily forget my engagements. Keep in mind that your church members will find it hard to overlook confusion or incompetence.

One of my most embarrassing moments came following the birth of our last child. We were in a new pastorate, having been there only four months when David was born. I had been invited by one of our church members to a fancy ladies' tea at an exclusive club in town. My folks were at my home to see their newest grandchild, and my daddy was with me when I realized I had forgotten the engagement. I shrieked, and said, "What in the world am I going to tell her?" He said, "Just the truth!" That was good advice, and even though I had excellent excuses, I felt guilty and irresponsible. I should have marked it down!

For another thing, writing responsibilities down enables us to see at a glance if we are evenly scheduled. I can look at Tuesday of next week and see if I'm going to be able to handle all the things I've written in. Some items will appear every day. We know what those are, but the extras trip us. Get ahead of your problems by figuring out what should be done now to insure smooth sailing later. If you teach Sunday School on Sunday, you have to make time for preparation. All these things need to be incorporated in the schedule. As they say, "The poorest pencil has a better memory than the sharpest mind." That's right, so write it down!

A third reason for keeping a calendar is that we can see with a quick look whether we are being good stewards of our time. Are we doing important things, or giving first-rate loyalty to second-rate causes? I've often wondered what I would have done had I not married and had a family. I don't know, but I am sure that having my feet under a bridge table all day would never have sufficed. I really want my life to count.

Writing it down makes us aware of putting first things first. Carolyn Weatherford Crumpler, former W.M.U. leader, says she ended every workday with making a list for the next day. One businessman said he set aside Friday afternoon for planning for the following week. Jackie Kennedy, regardless of what you think about her, is known to keep a list of tasks with her at all times. We often go shopping and forget one item, necessitating another trip. An ever-present list will save time and money.

One of our faculty wives says that before retiring on Sunday night she makes a grocery list for her Monday shopping. Prior to this, she plans meals for the week. This helps eliminate those extra trips to the store, which are expensive. Every time you go to the grocery store for three items you pick up ten. Lists have value.

Be realistic with your planning. Be realistic about your energy level, what your husband wants you to do or not do, how many children you have, and what you can handle. There is just so much any human can do, and we have to draw the line at some point.

It helps to know your personal rhythms of maximum effectiveness. We have daily, weekly, and monthly swings. They are different for each of us. Determine your prime time—morning or night.

Sometimes our swings have to do with biology. In fact, I learned a new word the other day. "Biochronology" is a study of time's relationship to biological processes. Know yourself. You are the one who has to schedule time in keeping with that knowledge. Decide if you are a racehorse or a turtle. Then order your life accordingly.

Although I live in New Orleans among night people, I don't belong to that group. I do my best work in the morning, so when afternoon comes, I'm no good. Prime activities demand prime time. Do your toughest and most distasteful jobs at that time.

You should plan time when you are available for other people. We can call it availability time. There are times when you need to be at home for your husband and your children. Many personal tasks can be done when the family is away during the day, giving you availability time at night. Don't plan to do ironing when the whole family is present. Don't make your telephone calls when you need to be available for others.

But leave some time for yourself too. Most of us fail to do that. This is "I" time. We need to plan "I" time, "we" time, and "family" time. Let's define these.

"I" time is that unstructured time when we can do what we like. Wives especially need it, but husbands need it too. Don't fuss if your husband wants to go fishing occasionally. He needs some "I" time. It slows me down just to read about God out walking in the cool of the day. If we are to be like Him, we must schedule leisure.

I have a niece who became a mother late in life. She married at thirty-one and had three kids in five years. When the first one came along, it was a miserable adjustment for her. I mean her whole schedule was shot. She had always set aside a cluster of time if she had something special to do. She looked at me one day in desperation and said, "Aunt Jo Ann, I don't *ever* get to do the things I have always done." Then, looking at her daughter as if it had just dawned on her, she remarked, "And she's not going anywhere!" I said, "No, Doll, she's not going anywhere for twenty or so years. You'd better get used to this."

One afternoon when her husband came in, she was in need of some "I" time. He walked in the door and she said, "Here! I'll be back." She handed him the baby and left. I later asked her, "Where did you go?" She replied, "Well, it sounds crazy, but I took the newspaper I had not read in weeks, and went to McDonald's."

"I" time—you need to plan it. You must have it to "play." I take that time for myself when I get two publications—*Guideposts* and *Good Housekeeping*. When these come, I treat myself to an hour or two of uninterrupted reading. Then I can face graciously some of those things I really don't want to do.

"We" time is scheduled time alone with your husband. I love my children, but there are times when my husband and I need to get away from them. I used to love those people who invited my children for social occasions with us. When you have four, people don't often include them. However, I also enjoyed the times when Landrum and I were invited alone. This gave us time for what I like to call "debriefing." "We" time can be lunch or supper together or even coffee if that is all the time you can manage. Failure to schedule couple time will prove extremely damaging to ministry and your marriage. As I mentioned at the outset of this chapter, lack of time together is one of the biggest "troublemakers" in marriage today.

Many times you need to get away from the family to evaluate the home situation. Sometimes I would have to go with Landrum on what I call one-night stands, when he was going out to preach and come right back. In the car we could talk about the kids and maybe some of the problems we were facing at the time.

"Family" time is when we are all together engaged in common activity. Someone said, "I try to spend some good time with my family, so I'm not forced to spend bad time with them." I expect there are families who have spent bad time with children as a result of failure to spend good time with them.

We have a preacher friend who just resigned from his church. He said, "You can talk about all the super churches you want to, but when your family is not functioning properly that all pales into insignificance." We need to remember that. I told Landrum a long time ago and have repeated it over and over again, "Honey, I don't care what you're elected to. I don't care what honors come to you in the Southern Baptist Convention or how many invitations you get to preach. If our kids don't turn out well, as far as I'm concerned, we've failed." We will have failed in the ministry closest to us. Our children *are* the Lord's work. They deserve our attention and our time—the availability time I mentioned earlier. It is essential to schedule family times.

I have never worked outside the home on a regular basis. Did you notice how I phrased that? People ask, "Mrs. Leavell, do you work?" and I always say no, but that's not altogether true. I have never really worked outside the home, yet I've worked a heap in it! They tell me it takes a housewife twelve hours to do what a working woman, a career woman, does in three and one-half. I know why! The housewife is not motivated to do her work in the least amount of time, because no one is checking on her. In business you are checked, or you don't get your check! There are some unfulfilled women working at home, not because they don't have a challenging task and ministry, but because they are not taking control. They fail to schedule themselves. They're not planning well.

Some people are practically born with the ability to plan and organize. The rest of us seem to be searching for misplaced articles from the beginning. Being organized is about 90 percent work and 10 percent talent, but will give us and our family a great sense of well-being.

Where do you start? Take a Sunday afternoon with two or three hours of uninterrupted time. Draw up a timetable of tasks, and enlist the help of family members to select areas of responsibility. Shared responsibility is often the answer to unorganized confusion.

There are things we have to do and things we want to do. If we finish the "have to's" in record time, and throw in a few "need to's," what do we have more time left to do? The "want to's"! We're not talking about saving time just for the fun of it. That's ridiculous. We are trying to do what we have to in record time in order to have time for the want to's, for "we" time, "family" time, and time for ministry beyond ourselves. Planning enables us to do more for ourselves and others.

Prioritize

What do we do after planning and enumerating? We prioritize. We list the things we've written down in order of their priority. Everything we need to do in a day's time is not of the same degree of importance. In fact, once we accomplish the first two out of ten items on our prioritized list, then we've already made a big dent in our tasks! The rest of the list actually goes easier this way.

What happens when you are interrupted? Do exactly as a doctor does when he has appointments and suddenly is called out to deliver a baby. Following the delivery, he goes back and picks up where he left off.

If we don't get to numbers eight, nine, and ten on a list, we can move them to the next day. We must prioritize. For our priorities to be right, our values must be right. Our priorities come from a sense of divine commission.

I've read that there are really four priorities: person, partner, parent, and public. Those are on target and easy to remember, as long as we understand that *the* priority comes before them all. We are familiar with the words of Jesus, "But seek ye first the kingdom of God, and His righteousness; and all these things shall be added to you" (Matthew 6:33). He is the One Who gives us the wisdom and direction to manage the other areas well.

It is so easy to run past God! The moment a Christian tries to direct his own paths, he steps down. We are promised in Proverbs 16:1, "Commit your work to the Lord, then it will succeed." If we know who we are as persons in Christ, we'll each make a much better person, a happy partner, a more influential parent, and the public will soon benefit from a life with predetermined plans and goals.

If you are in doubt about where your priorities are, ask yourself these questions:

What do I have time for?
What do I have money for?
What can interrupt me without my getting bent out of shape?

One of our trustees told about a boy who walked into a meeting his father was conducting with some business associates. The father *exploded* and shouted at him, "I've told you not to disturb me when

I'm in a meeting." The boy left and later that day took his own life in suicide. Apparently he had been feeling like a low priority for a long time.

We know another family who had an unwritten rule that the parents were not to be disturbed when at their vacation home off the Florida coast. That home has since disintegrated and it is little wonder with such misplaced priorities. Giving our children time now may be our best contribution to the next generation. I have found it helpful to get these couplets firmly in mind to establish my priorities:

People before things.
People before projects.
Family before friends.
Husband before children.
Husband before parents.
Tithe before wants.
Bible before opinions.
Jesus before *all*.

Divided loyalty is a problem for most of us. If we impress these guidelines into our minds, it will cut down on the anxiety which often accompanies tough decisions.

I try to practice what I preach. One morning Roland asked me if I would get him a yellow legal pad. With "people before projects" in mind, I decided to stop by the store on my way home from taking the kids to school, to buy the legal pad before I got busy for the day. I followed a group of people into the store, picked up the tablet, and proceeded to the cashier. This man looked at me in amazement and asked, "Lady, how did you get in? We are not even open." Evidently I had come in the employees' entrance. I shook the clerk up so badly that he told me if I had the correct change I could take my purchase. Landrum laughs and says I am the only woman alive who can even shop when the store is closed! But that was just due to my priorities.

Produce

"Do it, ditch it, or delegate it" was one person's advice. You see, being organized is not just notations on a calendar, but the self-discipline to make those marks reality. Someone said, "All worthwhile men have good thoughts, good ideas and good intentions—but precious few of them ever translate those into action."

Remember the equation: Bible study + application + *ministry* = spiritual fitness. My fear is many of us never get to the application or the "doing" of ministry. Do something—it is better to run in circles than sit still.

I've heard my husband describe the similarity between faith and the headlights of an automobile. As we begin to move, the lights illuminate the next step, not the end of the journey. In faith, we begin to operate on the light we already have and ask Him to reveal the next step.

I had a unique opportunity recently to speak to a group of senior citizens in one of our missions in New Orleans. A friend and I led the program together; she arranged several seasonal table settings as I talked about hospitality. One lady came to me as we concluded and said, "I wish I could get as excited as you all are over *something!*" I tried to be kind as I reminded her that often the excitement comes with the *doing*. The Lord Himself won't steer a stationary object!

Someone referred to me once as an "action-oriented achiever." I don't know about the achiever part, but I am action-oriented. I make no apology for that, because the happiest people I know are the busiest.

We as Baptists often get a lot of snide remarks about our activity. "You have to be in good physical condition to be a Baptist," they say. Activity is not the only evidence of the presence of the Holy Spirit, but it does seem He has plenty for us to do. The Scripture says Jesus Himself began "to do and to teach" and "went about doing good."

From the beginning God gave men and women a shared task. The *Covenant Marriage* material reminds us that Christian couples are called to be more than "an intimate twosome" or playmates. Family theorists suggest that "the relationship between persons has and needs a focus beyond the relationship itself." I'm told even the best of relationships fizzle if they are focused only on themselves and not the tasks before them.

"Love does not consist of looking at each other, but in looking outward together in the same direction" was one person's evaluation. As individuals and married partners, we must take seriously our call to minister and invest in the lives of others—"give back" what we have so generously been given.

We will never be like Him unless we manage our time and produce. Prioritize, then work your plan, and you will soon begin to feel a tremendous sense of accomplishment that will mean you won't *miss the blessing.*

CHAPTER 10

LOOK AROUND:
Hospitality

YOUR MINISTRY WILL BE greatly strengthened if you are "given to hospitality." Even if you don't feel gifted in this area, there are many people around to help you. I heard about a university without a president that sent a search committee to interview three men. When the committee went to visit one of these, the candidate's wife told them right away, "If you are expecting me to do any entertaining, forget it!" I not only thought that was poor judgment, but she was limiting her husband's ministry. His chances of being considered after that were slim to none. Had he accepted such a post, she could have arranged to have her job done.

You don't have to do everything yourself. There are people around who will help you with your parties. At our seminary there are many faculty wives who are more than happy to assist me, and they do each time we have a reception. There are people in your church eager to join in, just waiting to be asked.

Don't limit yourself and your husband by saying hospitality is not your gift. This is something that can be learned and enjoyed. If you practice being hospitable, it is a wonderful channel for ministry.

There are two main things to think about regarding hospitality. First you must decide to extend it to others, and then you must pay attention to the details of entertaining in order to pull it off successfully. So let's explore these points.

Make the Decision

The first requirement is a *decision* to be hospitable. Someone observed, "Children are growing up today not even knowing the dining room table has leaves." There is very little entertaining going on in our homes today. I don't know what kind of home you grew up in or how much hospitality was extended, but let me ask you this: How long has it been since you invited friends into your home? It may have been a while since you were entertained in a home yourself. Most of the time we take guests out.

We spend a lifetime accumulating things for dinner parties. We can't wait to get our silver, china, and crystal—all those lovely wedding gifts that are now collecting dust. When the opportunity presents itself to have people in our home, we refuse or cop out by going to a restaurant.

Landrum and I go to a lot of different churches now. By virtue of Landrum's position at the seminary, he often preaches in a different church every Sunday. He has also served as interim pastor for a number of churches. We are entertained by lots of people, but seldom in homes. Let me tell you at the outset, I think the sweetest fellowship of all is around a table in your home. I *beg* my family to sit around the table after a meal. My favorite spot in any home is the kitchen. No room in the house spoons out as much support and love as it does.

Several years ago we served as interim at the Dawson Memorial Baptist Church in Birmingham. We had wonderful fellowship. A hospitality committee assigned us to different families in the church every week. Many of them had us in their homes, more than I ever remember experiencing. The hosts were of all ages. We got acquainted with many young couples with growing families, but one of the neatest couples who entertained us in their home were senior citizens. They had lived in a retirement community but didn't like it. What they missed most there was children. They left the retirement center, came back to Birmingham, moved into a single-family dwelling, and prepared a meal for us in their home. Don't you wish for that sort of spunk in your senior years? I enjoyed it.

I don't know what has been more spiritually meaningful in my life recently than those months in Birmingham. Landrum and I cherish the friendships we made during that time and I got more new recipes! However, what I remember most were those individuals who took the time to make a contribution to our lives. A life-style that includes others requires a *decision* on your part to be hospitable.

Did you grow up in a family with frequent guests, or did you grow up in a family without many get-togethers? My big family was around a lot, but I don't remember many outsiders being invited into our home. One day when my mother was at my home, she heard me telephoning guests for a dinner party. After I had made several calls she said, "Jo Ann, what are you going to have?" I said, "I don't know, but if I get them invited I'll think of something!" There was a look of horror on her face and she replied, "Well, I believe I would think of what I was going to have before I invited them." I said, "That is why you never have company." Don't wait for perfect conditions before being hospitable. Jump in there.

I am not suggesting you invite a bunch of people and never give it any thought. What I am saying is that it requires a decision. Pick next Thursday night or Friday night, and *decide* you are going to be hospitable toward somebody—some couple, family, or friend. Most of us perform better under pressure anyway, so make a firm decision to put hospitality into practice.

I'm told 80 percent of the entertaining being done is because we "have to." I *have* to give two graduation receptions every year. Other entertaining is necessary, but don't merely do what you are required to do.

Set a time and do it just because you want to be obedient. The Bible says, "Share with God's people who are in need. Practice hospitality" (Romans 12:13). I am talking about a biblical admonition here.

Don't just set a time, but do it "without grumbling." I get so tired of hearing people fuss about company, gripe about relatives who come to visit, and complain about all their responsibilities. Do you hear some of this? In the beauty shop, you can hear women complaining, "Well, my children have been here *all* week." The Scripture says we are to practice hospitality without grumbling. "For it is God Who works in you to will and to act according to His good purpose. Do everything without complaining or arguing" (Philippians 2:13-14). We often feel sorry for ourselves, and put upon. We indulge in self-pity and this is contagious—to our children. They will pick up this attitude, and I don't believe the inhospitable atmosphere is what we want to perpetuate.

Gracious entertaining is an art, just as surely as painting a picture. No doubt you have been in other homes where you felt *most* uncomfortable. When you feel that way, chances are you will never go back. It all has to do with the hostess's attitude.

I am never happier than when I am on the active end of hospitality. Every time I am busy preparing for guests, I think of Martha. Mary sat at Jesus's feet, and Martha was working in the kitchen "grumbling" because Mary wasn't helping her. Martha's problem does not seem to be her serving as much as her attitude.

I have always been a Martha to the point that whenever I hear a sermon on that passage of Scripture I get a guilty conscience. I finally decided some years ago I was just going to be a "happy" Martha. The world would be in sad shape without a few of us to serve tables—especially in our Baptist churches! The key to whether or not you enjoy hospitality is found at this point—attitude.

It might help if we remember the subtle difference between hospitality and entertaining. The best definition I've found is in Gail MacDonald's book, *High Call, High Privilege.*

> Hospitality is a safe place, entertainment is a show place. Hospitality focuses on people, entertainment focuses on things. Hospitality creates an open atmosphere, entertainment can be neat and closed. Hospitality exudes a warm attitude, entertainment can degenerate to being cool and calculating. Hospitality puts one at ease, entertainment implies competition.

The hospitable entertaining I am talking about is not this showy kind of entertainment. Hospitality is not for show but is an atmosphere you provide. It occurs when you are more concerned with the people than what you are serving. You are more interested in your guests than whether everything is in perfect order in your home. Britannica Dictionary says to be hospitable is to be "disposed to behave in a warm manner or to entertain with generous kindness." This is the attitude I pray you will cultivate. Otherwise you will *miss the blessing!*

The problem is that our emphasis usually centers on self rather than on others. If we can shift gears from concern for self to the importance of the guests in our homes, we won't have to work at being hospitable. Practice that spirit and see what a difference it makes.

Let's look at some reasons for our failure to open our homes. Probably the biggest and most important factor is a lack of confidence. You lack even more confidence if you did not grow up in a family where having company was commonplace. If you were raised helping a mother who had frequent guests, you will already enjoy an expertise that others have to develop. My daughter, ever since she could reach the sink, has helped me make sandwiches for Sunday night company. She has helped me prepare for any number of guests in our home, and I treasure those moments of kitchen talk. Ann can entertain now as well as I can, because she grew up with it.

What Landrum and I miss most from the pastorate are those Sunday night fellowships. Landrum always said that was his favorite time of the week, with sermons completed prior to beginning a new round of preparation. We literally fed the five thousand at those gatherings. Many is the night we had twenty-five adults and an equal number of children. I took it as a compliment when Lan, even as a teenager, would check with us before making his plans. He usually wanted to be a part of what we were doing. One of the greatest memories we can give our children is to have them share our table and be exposed to home-centered hospitality. Their own confidence for extending hospitality will build.

If you lack confidence, don't wait to be comfortable. Ease comes with time. Most of the worthwhile things we attempt are difficult before they are easy. If you see someone who is a pro at a task, you can know it hasn't always been that way. Find an individual who sings beautifully and you are confident it came with practice. If you see a person comfortable with entertaining, he or she has probably been at it awhile. Whatever the job, ease comes with practice. Make a decision to get involved and it will become easier. Put aside pride and allow yourself a few mistakes. No one is perfect.

The first barrier to extending hospitality is lack of confidence. Another barrier is money. We say it costs too much. It does cost; there is no question about that. Yet you do not have to pay back invitations in kind. If somebody has you for supper and you cannot really afford to have them for supper, invite them for dessert. It is not necessary to serve a twelve-course meal every time you have someone in your home. You don't have to spend a week's pay.

Our seminary cookbook, *Baptist Dishes Worth Blessing* (published by Pelican Publishing Company), has a good section on making plans for company. You can budget and buy food items over a period of weeks. If you plan wisely and space it out, you can have guests frequently on a limited income. We've done it! People are really more hungry for fellowship than they are for food anyway. You do not have to provide expensive food. Hospitality is more than a big meal—it is simply providing a friendly, comfortable atmosphere for your guests. Most of us have found that serving some food or drink helps create this warmth, but elaborate refreshments are not essential.

Let your guests participate by bringing a dish. We live in a day when this is appropriate. If somebody calls and invites you to a get-together on Friday night, it is now common to ask, "What do you want me to bring?" And when others offer to contribute food, take them up on it. Tell them to bring a salad, dessert, bread, chips and dip, or whatever you need. They will be happy to share the cost.

Time, or lack of it, is another excuse for failing to be hospitable. You will never "find" time; you've got to make it. If you are looking for a reason *not* to entertain, one is available. Every stage of life has its excuses. Now you may be saying, "My apartment is not nice enough. We just married and it is sparse." The next stage is, "Well, maybe when these kids get out of the way. I can't entertain now because of them." Do you know what my age group says? "Well, we travel too much," or "I used to do that, but I can't seem to get around to it anymore." Every age has its own rationale.

It's been written that "God is not looking for super stars, He is simply looking for availability." If you are available, you can find the time. You may say, "I am too tired, especially after I work all day." Often that is true, but do you know there is something refreshing about fellowship? I can be dragging physically, but after a period of fellowship I often feel refreshed. The Scripture says, "I can do all things through Christ which strengtheneth me" (Philippians 4:13). Why not claim that for yourself? It also says, "Let us not be weary in well doing" (Galatians 6:9). Don't indulge in self-pity and let your attitude get bad. Remember: you will *never* give out more than the Lord gives back!

If you practice hospitality, there will be interruptions in your schedule. This quality of fellowship and love is best illustrated in the parable of the good Samaritan. He was going along his way and was interrupted. He gave, it cost him, and it shot his schedule! You are going to plan some periods of hospitality, but at other times you are going to stumble upon need. There are wounded people all about us who need the ministry of a good Samaritan. Let me give you a case in point.

I had a girl in my Sunday School class who had one child, and right on the heels of that one she had twins. She had three babies under two years of age. I remember visiting her one morning on my way to a Sunday School luncheon. As a dutiful teacher I went by to see my pupil. I walked into her house, which was a *disaster*. She was still in bed from delivering her twins, and here were these three crying babies. Guess what I did? I patted her on the back, told her we had been thinking about her, and marched right out to my luncheon. If I had it to do over, I would have forgotten the luncheon. She needed *help*. I wasn't willing at that time to have my schedule interrupted. If we're truly hospitable, we'll be interested in people and their needs.

Hospitality is really a gift from one person to another. I could have given my friend something that day she would never have forgotten, and it wouldn't have cost me a thing but a little time. That failure has haunted me all these years. Have you found yourself in situations like that? I hope we will become more concerned about people than schedules, or we will miss the blessing.

Anything worthwhile is demanding. Hospitality is worthwhile and takes some confidence, money, and time. The demands are strenuous, and the lazy person will never get around to entertaining. Make the decision to accept these demands, for you and those around you will be richly rewarded.

Taking Care of Details

The next question is, "How can extending true hospitality best be accomplished?" We have already discussed how hospitality centers on the guests, not the food. *The important thing is not what is on the table, but who occupies the chairs.* With that fact always in mind, let me offer some guidelines.

No matter what the event—a formal dinner or family get-to-gether—making your guests feel relaxed and comfortable requires preparation. If the effort is organized, accomplishment will follow. Waiting till the last minute usually results in chaos. I visited a home once where the hostess went shopping for groceries after our arrival. It made us wonder how welcome we were and how much heart she had for our visit.

One of my first attempts at being organized for more than one meal at a time was when Landrum's sister, brother-in-law, and their children came to visit us for a week when we lived on the Mississippi Gulf Coast. I had no help. I had small children. I suddenly thought this would be a disaster if I didn't do some planning. I planned my meals, baked cookies and desserts for the freezer, and worked out meals for the whole week. My early preparation paid off. That was one of the most delightful weeks that I have ever experienced, simply because I had planned ahead.

Does it make you as nervous as it does me if the hostess constantly jumps up and down during a meal to take care of things? That really stems from a lack of preparation. If she has planned ahead, she can enjoy her guests. As they say, "At least 90 percent of our failure is due to a lack of organization." Careful planning and attention to details are the keys to the success of any party.

Let me mention some of the details that need to be taken care of if we are going to be hospitable and do it acceptably. There are certain rules and ways to do it right. I hope you will *master the basics.* For many, this will be second nature. Others will have to work at observing these rudiments.

Before you think this is unimportant, let me ask this question. If you were going to a foreign country as a missionary, what is the first thing you would do? You would learn the customs as well as what offends and what doesn't. This is why we send missionary appointees for four months of orientation. During this time they are learning acceptable ways to minister in a different culture.

We learn the rules of entertainment for the same reason. When we don't play by the rules of our culture, we offend. This causes people to look at us and think, "Neither that preacher nor his wife know the social graces," or "That woman in church cares very little about others."

My son-in-law grew up in a home that not only didn't practice hospitality, but did not know the basics. His mother was from another culture. She did not cook. If a child got hungry, that one went in the kitchen and made a sandwich. This is how Finis grew up.

He was a wonderful tennis player. He went to the state finals in Texas his junior year in high school. Do you know how he learned his table manners? He was smart enough to observe others as he traveled with the tennis team.

That should convince you to master the basics, so let's look at them. For one thing, many people don't know how to set a table. They think this is no big deal, but I read, "The one who sets the table is second in importance only to the cook." There are those in your church who will expect you to know how to set a table.

I was in a church at a ladies' banquet recently. The tables were not set properly. They had the knives and forks on the wrong side. I can guarantee there were people present, other than I, who knew the difference.

I have been through it with cafeteria managers. I went in the cafeteria one night just before a big banquet. The tables were completely set up, but incorrectly. The salad was on the right, the coffee cup on the left, and it went downhill from there. I stopped someone who was setting the last of the tables and said, "Oh, honey, the coffee cup goes on the right." She replied, "Oh, it doesn't matter." I said, "Oh, but it does."

We did not have time that night to change it, but I can assure you it didn't happen again. I made a diagram of a correct table setting and hung it in the cafeteria. You *must* play by the rules. Place knives, sharp edge toward plate, and spoons at the right of the plate. Forks are placed at the left. Silverware is placed from the outside in as it will be used. The napkin's folded edge goes toward the plate on the left by the forks. Glasses go directly above the knife and spoon. If a salad plate is used, it is placed to the left of the forks. Learn to set a table properly so when guests arrive, you don't have to worry about anything but friends and food.

Plan seating if there are more than four people. If you have just one other couple, it is not necessary, but if you have a larger group, you must think through it ahead of time. This is in order to make everyone comfortable. Put together people who have common interests. We took thirteen people out to supper recently to be with the Dan Vestals, who were guests on campus. I had worked out the seating ahead of time on paper and brought it in my pocket. I wanted the people who had not been with the Vestals to be close enough to visit. We had one other new couple with us and I wanted them to be where they would meet people. Seating must be planned to accomplish the purpose for your gathering.

If you have a lack of space, you may want to plan a buffet. If you don't have a buffet but are serving the food, you serve from the left side of a guest's plate. If you are passing a bowl, you pass to the left side. Why? Most people are right-handed, and they can reach over and spoon out the food. There are reasons for these rules.

If you are removing the plate, you remove from the right. So remember: serve from the left and remove from the right. And, as a guest, never leave a spoon in a bowl or a cup. This is a common mistake.

Here are some more pointers for guests. If you are given a steak, it is impolite to cut the whole steak. Cut one bite at a time. We get in the habit, when our children are small, of completely cutting up something for them. This is not done in polite company with adults. Also, use good judgment and consider the portions you take. Have you been behind people in a buffet line or at the table who took half a casserole and there were six other people to be served?

Toothpicks are one of my pet peeves. Nothing shows a lack of good breeding as quickly as public use of a toothpick. When Landrum and I were dating, we would leave a restaurant and he would get a toothpick. I would think, "My word, his mother must not have taught him anything!" I was relieved the first time I was around her and she fussed at him about his toothpick. I told her, "Oh, I am so glad you did not teach him that." She assured me she didn't. I think my boys use a toothpick to aggravate me. I want to put a sign on them that says, "My mother tried to teach us better!" It absolutely drives me up the wall, and if there is anything worse than a man using one, it is a woman. A lady will *never* be seen with a toothpick.

My whole family knows how I feel about toothpicks. David had a new girlfriend not long ago. He brought her to Lisa's home, our daughter-in-law. When I talked with Lisa, I asked her what she thought of David's new girl. She said, "She is all right." I knew she didn't sound excited. I asked her to tell me a little more about her. She said, "Mom, you don't need to worry about her. When she picked up a toothpick, I knew it would never work!"

Now let's turn our attention to the atmosphere of your party, beginning with clothing. When you extend invitations, specify dress. People appreciate that. Nothing destroys your confidence like appearing at a function overdressed or underdressed. Landrum gave the benediction at a gathering recently, and he was the *only* man not dressed in formal attire. It didn't bother him, but I would have been devastated!

A fun thing to do is decorate the house. You might want to put a bow or balloons on the front door, if you are having a party. Any extra touch tells guests they are welcome.

Turn the lights down. You can't see the dust as well when the lights are low! Put on soft music. Fragrance is important for a party too. There is something about a pleasant smell that is inviting. I love to serve hot wassail because it makes the house smell *wonderful.*

Finally, let's think about the menu. Plan your food as carefully as you do your guest list. A simple menu that does not require last-minute preparation is probably best. Using familiar, proven recipes will contribute to your confidence and make you a more relaxed hostess. This is not the time for new recipes. They are fun and will keep your cooking fresh, but I would not suggest you use them on first-time company.

Landrum's sister has kept a consistent list through the years of menus and guests in her home. This is invaluable in preventing duplication of menus to the same people over a period of time.

Give attention to color, nutrition, and budget when planning your meal. Using in-season food will cut down on cost, and fruit is always appropriate and appreciated—especially for dieters! Whatever your choice is for your guests, just have *plenty.* Few things are worse than skimpy portions served with a penurious spirit. Haven't you been exposed to this spirit? We have—where it seems taking a second helping would encroach on the next day's allotment! It is not required that you have three meats and six vegetables, but serve plenty of what you do have. If you are willing to share with others, the Lord *does* provide.

A sense of humor is always useful to a nervous hostess. You will have some catastrophes. *Don't panic.* Just laugh if anything goes wrong. Mistakes can become fond memories.

I remember my first stab at entertaining when we came to the seminary. I was planning to have banana splits for the student wives organization. The biggest attendance they had ever had for a meeting at that time was seventy. I took into consideration that a few more might show up to check out this new president's wife, so I made two hundred and ten ice cream balls. My logic was that if seventy came they could each have three scoops, but if a hundred came I would just tell them to have two. Pretty smart, huh? To further complicate this, I was speaking to them that night on "Entertaining in the Pastorium." I quickly changed my subject to "How *Not* to Panic when You Entertain in the Pastorium," because I quit counting after a hundred and thirty guests streamed into my home. My husband went to the store for more ice cream and bananas, and we multiplied the loaves and fishes. We had a *wonderful* time, but I'll have to admit I have never cleaned up a stickier mess!

Making a time list may avoid other embarrassments. I have even changed my menu after making such a list when it became obvious I had too many dishes requiring oven use. Writing down your schedule will usually help clear up other problem areas also.

Something I have found useful is to wait awhile before serving dessert. This does several things. Since most of us have no help, it moves our guests away from the dirty dishes to another room in the home. I've seen this work even in a small seminary apartment. It also mixes up our visitors and prolongs the evening of fellowship. Otherwise, we eat the full meal in one place, mix very little, and the long evening can become a drag—especially if conversation lags.

If you have a long guest list, you might want to consider a party on two consecutive nights. We had too many deacons in Wichita Falls for me to serve comfortably in our home, but I wanted to heed my mother-in-law's advice to "always have your deacons!" I wanted to include their wives, which presented an even bigger problem. We finally picked out three nights in one week, divided our guest lists, served the same menu, and had a wonderful time of food and fellowship. These are just some of the details that should be taken care of, and they will make your hospitality that much more enjoyable to your guests.

More Hospitable Hints

Above all, don't neglect yourself. Your mood sets the atmosphere for your gathering, and you will never overcome negligence at this point. I learned this the hard way! If you are not dressed and ready at the appointed time, your guests will go unattended and your poise will be *shot*. You can enlist help from others if you are running behind in your last-minute preparation. Believe me, this is the way to go.

Progressive suppers can be good mixers for a large group. We have had these frequently in the Sunday School classes I have taught. The first thing this does is involve more hostesses. Anytime I have been able to get others to open their homes it has been an encouragement to me. The greatest favor you may do another is to give her a taste of the joy that accompanies the open door. I've even asked some to participate. The most reluctant ones were usually the ones who thanked me the most for giving them the opportunity to be hospitable.

We frequently had our progressive suppers at Christmastime and went house to house on the church bus, stopping for appetizers, salad, the main course, and dessert. These gatherings could usually warm up the coldest heart as we fellowshipped and carolled, viewing the beautiful Christmas lights. What better way to involve some fringe members of your class or church.

The most useful advice I can offer if your best-laid plans fail to materialize was given me years ago by a helper. I would begin to worry, and ask, "Do you think we are going to make it? Do you think we are going to be ready on time?" Her answer was always the same: "Just keep a-working, just keep a-working." If we do that, I can promise delight will always follow faithfulness.

Satisfaction has come to me in many ways because of the hospitality I have provided. Aside from being obedient, training children, and developing friendship, I think the greatest blessing comes from using your home as a redemptive agent in the world. God will not let any of your loving acts or words go to waste. If you are a mother, you have numerous opportunities to influence other people's children. Parents are truly missionaries, beginning with daily relationships. I think of the hundreds of young people I have fed—some staying as long as two weeks, and of all races and nationalities.

When our daughter was a freshman at Baylor she brought home eight girls for Mardi Gras. They stayed for five days, and Landrum says you haven't *lived* until you have shared a bathroom situation with eight girls! Curlers were everywhere.

Our boys especially have always brought home the "strays." I'm constantly reminded of the Scripture that tells us we may be "entertaining angels unaware!" Who knows, the time may come when one of your children will be in desperate need of someone practicing the admonition to be hospitable.

One supper club Landrum and I were involved in bears mention here. Together with three other couples, we planned a dinner monthly, inviting four other couples who needed the Lord or the ministry of our church. The hosts did the inviting, and we made the numbers equal so nobody would feel intimidated or strange—eight of us and eight prospects. It turned out to be a wonderful tool for outreach. Many people will come to your home who would *never* accept an invitation to church. We enlisted everyone of those whom we entertained, and I'm just naive enough to believe the Lord honored our efforts at being hospitable.

Pray He will use you to have a positive influence over everyone who crosses your threshold. Wouldn't it be great if someone found Christ at your table?

Have you neglected this all-important area of influence? If so, realign your priorities. Make that decision to be hospitable, entertain with an eye for the details, and *don't miss the blessing.*

CHAPTER 11

LOOK AROUND:
Hospitality in Writing

A FACET OF HOSPITALITY can be shared with pen, paper, and stamps. Someone has called this "handwritten hugs that encircle what arms can't reach."

I have to be honest up front and tell you I did not grow up a letter-writer. I wasn't really taught to send thank-you notes. I am sure my mother, on rare occasions, made me write them. Don't all mothers? However, it wasn't a habit for me until I married into the Leavell family.

I observed my mother-in-law during her visits with us. She would write notes the whole time to family and friends—notes of encouragement, sympathy, counsel, or appreciation. After her visit, she would go home and write people in our town who had been especially kind to her. She might write the music director and thank him for his music. She would write those who took her out to lunch or entertained and befriended her.

I am slow in a lot of ways, but I began to put two and two together. I observed people as they warmed up to her. I have since called hospitality in writing the best "friend-maker" in the world. A thank-you note will go a long way toward endearing you to your church people. It will create unparalleled goodwill. I want you to know how to do it and do it *well*.

If you have not grown up writing notes, this will not come easily. Go ahead and do it anyway, because you will improve with practice. The only way to become good at writing notes is to do it.

If you are a preacher's wife, hospitality in writing will be a tremendous help to you in ministry. I do not believe a thank-you note in the mail-out bulletin at Christmastime is sufficient when people have been so incredibly generous to the pastor and his wife. Those kindnesses deserve a personal touch. Even if you are not married to a minister, proper recognition of the support you receive from other church members is still a good Christian practice. Let me suggest several things.

Eight Tips for Writing Notes

First, put words on paper *exactly* as you would say them in conversation. I have heard notes referred to as "written conversation." I like that. The words have to *sound* like you.

Look at this note I received recently:

Jo Ann,

Thank you very much for the baby gift.

Juanita

If you had received that note, would you think your gift was very much appreciated? I don't think so. It is perhaps better than nothing, but truly has very little to commend it. The gift was not described in any way. She didn't mention color or how it was going to be used. There was nothing of a personal nature in that note. A good letter is one which reflects the specialness of the receiver and the personality of the writer.

I would rather get a letter from my sister-in-law than eat when I am hungry. She is darling and writes just exactly as she talks. I have entertained my friends for years with letters from Margaret. They are a scream, and reflect her personality. Write letters that reflect *your* uniqueness.

Second, your note paper will tell a great deal about you. Stick to simple stationery in good taste. I will give you my preference, but it is not binding for you. I don't care for paper with "thank you" printed on the front. I would rather have plain white note paper with a deckle edge. If you can spend more money, print notes with your monogram on the front. Even note paper reflects your personality. In a sense your note paper is an accessory, like scarves and jewelry are to your appearance. It also says you care enough for the receiver to put a little expense and added thought into this note.

I prefer good paper over cards with printed messages inside. If you are just learning to express yourself in writing you may want to send a card, but add a personal word. Nothing reaches individuals more than a personal, handwritten note.

Someone has called greeting cards "our emotional fast food . . . precooked apologies, flash frozen congratulations, preshrunk expressions of sympathy." These are tough words, but true. The telephone and greeting cards have dealt letter writing a blow. What is the advantage of a letter or a note over a phone call? You can open it, read it and reread it, remember exactly what it said, and perhaps on occasion pass it on to future generations. I have letters in my children's baby books that I have passed on and I can already see how they continue to bless.

When my grandson, Roland Quinche Leavell III, was born, Roland and Lisa used a special quote on the front of the baby announcement. It was from a letter written thirty years before when the baby's father was born. This was only possible because those thoughts had been put in writing.

When my mother-in-law died, I fell heir to a box of stuff. I brought it home and promptly put it in my attic. Not long ago I took that big box to sort through. In there she had kept every Valentine card we had ever sent her, every Mother's Day card, even those pitiful little thank-you notes my kids had written. She had lovingly preserved them. I divided them, and I have a package for all four of my children. I hope they appreciate them as much as I did. Can you see what those written remembrances meant to her? Don't neglect sending these "handwritten hugs," and remember that a personally written note on tasteful stationery will probably be more cherished than a store-bought greeting card.

Third, your attitude will come through in the notes you write. If you view notes and letters as a chore, that attitude will be detected. Juanita's note came through as a chore. It was obvious she felt she had to do it. She was getting rid of her obligation the quickest way possible.

I really think we can have fun writing notes if we have a positive attitude toward them. One way to do that is picture yourself on the receiving end of those notes. How many times have you been encouraged by someone's letter? I have a folder of notes I have received through the years. If I ever get really low, I can go to that file, read those notes, and come alive because of the thoughtfulness of someone with a positive attitude toward letter writing.

Fourth, *never* begin a note with "thank you." When you do, it is immediately apparent it is just a plain ole thank-you note. The receivers will look at the signature, but that is about all they are going to see or remember. Try to include a paragraph about something other than the gift or dinner. It doesn't matter what it is—the people's home, their children, or the party's menu. Anything of a personal nature will do.

Fifth, include the name of the giver somewhere in the body of the material, if possible. "Sister, I love the sweater you gave me." "Ann, the meal was wonderful." This makes the note much more personal.

Sixth, don't let bad grammar or poor spelling hinder you. I know that all of us have not been blessed with a good background in grammar and spelling. However, the dictionary can help you. I seldom write notes without going to the dictionary to check a word.

Several years ago we had a Woman's Conference on campus. Ann Kiemel Anderson, a well-known author, was one of our speakers. I wrote a note to assure her we were looking forward to her coming. I was using a word I didn't know how to spell. I left it blank and was going to look it up. Of course I mailed the letter and never once thought of the blank until later. I sat down two or three days later, confessed my negligence in another note to her, and made a joke out of it. I figured she had probably done the same thing before. Use the dictionary, or think of another word. Don't let these uncertainties stop you from writing.

Seventh, I think plenty of dots, dashes, and underlinings make a letter interesting. Use all of the attention-getting devices available. These reflect true emotions, which mean more to the recipient than getting a letter that's perfect in every way. Exclamation marks in a note can lend excitement. Several question marks can get across the fact that you are bewildered about something. Use imaginative punctuation that reflects your personality.

Finally, pay attention to the note's form. Juanita's note did not include any sort of salutation. Many people make this mistake. They just say "Jo Ann" or "Mrs. Leavell," and never start with "Dear." The good traditional form requires the use of "Dear" plus the name. If it is someone who is familiar to you, use the first name. If you are not comfortable with a first name, just say "Dear Friend." In the body of the letter you may use the name, but have some sort of salutation. Start the body of the letter a few spaces below. Sign off with a closing, followed by a comma when you get to the end. Don't just write "Juanita," but "Love, Juanita" if you know them well.

However, don't use "Love" unless you mean it. It could be misinterpreted. "Sincerely" is always appropriate, or "Affectionately" if you know them a little better. Then comes your name. I always sign my first name. I would never sign as "Mrs. Jo Ann Leavell." If necessary, I will put "Mrs." in parentheses, or I will put "Jo Ann Leavell" and sign "Mrs. Landrum Leavell" underneath.

"Mrs." really should be used with your husband's name. Landrum is picky about this also. He says I am either Mrs. Landrum Leavell, or I am Jo Ann Leavell, but I am not Mrs. Jo Ann Leavell. This is just one of "our" peculiarities. He does a slow burn when I am listed as Mrs. Jo Ann Leavell in the bulletin.

I have a "thing" about the use of "Ms." when addressing notes. I have used it because divorce has created its own set of problems. If I don't know if somebody is divorced, if they have ever been married, or if I am not familiar with the situation, I will use it as a last resort.

Thoughts about
Your Written Thoughts

Those are the eight main suggestions I have to offer on hospitality in writing. They are good guidelines for getting you started in this valuable practice. I also have a few more bits of advice for you as you continue in this pursuit.

I often write my notes off on a scratch pad first. It may seem like double trouble but it works for me. If I am sitting with good paper in hand, I waste time fearing I'll make a mistake and hesitating to begin. When I jot the notes off and copy them later, fear is removed.

Include clippings or cartoons if that reflects your personality. My sister-in-law never sends a letter without including something she thinks would be of interest to us.

If your note asks for a recipe, or has any other similar request, include a self-addressed envelope. This is the least you can do if you are asking a favor.

If you have several notes to send, I learned a tip from my oldest son. When Lan was a seminary student in New Orleans, I observed him addressing and stamping numerous envelopes after spending a weekend back at his church. As time permitted during the week he would write letters to those who had entertained him or others who needed a note of encouragement. He told me this routine worked best for him. I have developed this habit now and heartily recommend it. It may be all in my mind, but once the notes are addressed and stamped, it seems half the work is done.

Set a deadline for sending thank-you notes. In our last pastorate people were wonderfully thoughtful toward us at Christmastime. At the end of the holidays, I was almost overwhelmed with all those notes I needed to write. My experience taught me the importance of a self-imposed deadline. I would try to write ten notes a day, just as a bride does after the honeymoon. Set yourself some limits; don't let it sap your energy for months. Do it, and the sooner the better.

On occasion you might want to send a second thank-you note at some future time. If somebody has been really good to you, you might send another note about a month after your initial one. The surprises of life are memorable. If you can think of some way to thank people that is just a little bit different, you will make their day. I am not saying write a note or two every time you are in a home in your church family. You are going to have a few people who have you over frequently. Vary your thanks. If you have written them, you might want to call them next time. You might send them a little gift or let your husband express gratitude for a change. I am not saying he can't help you, but I don't think you ought to leave it all up to him, and I don't think he ought to leave it all up to you. These are things we share.

Most importantly, train your children to write notes. You'll do them a tremendous disservice if you don't teach them early to express appreciation. There are lots of ways you can encourage note writing even when the children are little. You can write the note and let them draw a picture on it or sign it. Try to make them very familiar with the habit of sending messages.

Dear Abby says, "A simple thank you is not too much to expect in return for a gift. Show me a person who for the sheer joy of giving continues to give to someone who shows no sign of appreciation." I know this by experience. We had a deacon who was incredibly good to us and our staff. One time he said to my husband, "Do you know I have never gotten a note of appreciation from so-and-so? I just want to tell you I am through!" After his repeated kindnesses this negligence was inexcusable.

People need to know you are appreciative, so be sure to demonstrate hospitality in writing. Using my pointers above, set an example for others in your church, or for the next preacher's wife. She is going to come along behind you and reap what you have sowed. If you are a minister's wife, you either leave a bad taste in the mouths of your church members or you leave a good one. What reputation will you leave?

Don't just write notes; go back to writing full-fledged letters. Letter writers, like families, have become an endangered species. I hope you write your parents. I am on the other side of the fence now. I love to get letters from my children. My husband was one-of-a-kind, writing to his mother every Monday morning. If he was leaving for a revival on Monday, he wrote her Sunday night, or Sunday afternoon from the church. That was his ritual, and she watched for that letter. I also wrote her. I felt she wanted to hear from me also because women tell different things. I would tell all the details of the family, and Landrum would tell the Sunday School attendance!

Let's go back to showing appreciation in writing. It is a wonderful thing to practice, and my guidelines above should help you in this endeavor. *Don't miss this blessing.*

CHAPTER 12

LOOK AROUND:
Money

LET'S TAKE A SERIOUS LOOK at money. It is a special concern for ministers' families because of limited income, and because it is a material matter in a spiritual life-style. However, since any Christian woman can be subject to these same problems with money, an examination of its management should benefit all of us.

I am going to be honest with you—money management is not my long suit. My daddy was a banker and I must have somehow thought I was just going to absorb all that knowledge. When my husband and I married, I had never worked, never earned a dime in my life, but I thought I was a financial genius. It has not worked out that way!

I must be like my mother, because I certainly don't "take after" my daddy. I have a sister who worked in a bank—she probably got all his genes.

One day after we had talked about money in class, I had a student wife tell me, "Mrs. Leavell, I don't really think you understand our situation." All I can say to you is, "I do understand." We began marriage without any financial assistance. Landrum was from a Baptist preacher's home full of love but little money. My folks were more comfortable, but they had a conviction that when you married, you were on your own. Unlike young couples today, we did not get help from anyone.

We promptly moved to Charleston, Mississippi, after the wedding, a little north Mississippi town where Landrum had become pastor three months before our marriage. We loved Mississippi, and Landrum still thinks a minister's education has not been complete if he has not pastored in that state. He is really grieved that two of our boys, our oldest son and our son-in-law, have not served as pastor of a church in Mississippi. However, David was recently called to a country church where Landrum was pastor in the fifties. That has been a neat experience, with father and son comparing the past and present. Mississippi was good to us, especially Charleston, where I went as a twenty-one-year-old bride.

Landrum's salary was not large, but when we were first married we didn't spend a lot. Nearly four years later we moved to Gulfport, Mississippi, where we served seven years, and the financial crunch started. When we left Gulfport, we received $9,600 a year plus a place to live. That was not much money for a family with three children and a fourth on the way.

We then spent eleven years in Wichita Falls. Of course expenses increased during that time, but our salary did not. We were in one of the ten largest churches in the Southern Baptist Convention, but the salary barely paid the bills. Not all large churches pay large salaries, but we look back and marvel at the way God supplied our needs and many of our wants. The memory of generous church members still blesses us, but there are memories of hard times also.

There were a lot of things we didn't have. I tell my kids that now is the first time we have ever had two dimes to rub together that were not already committed. It is nice not to be so pressed and to have all tuition bills behind us for the first time. Maybe from this you can grasp that I do understand. I've been there.

I can remember some of those money discussions. You know the kind. If I live to be a *hundred,* I will never forget one of those in the parking lot at the church, of all places. Why Landrum picked that place to decide we couldn't spend any more money at Christmas I'll never know. I must have been shopping. I had gone by the church to show my purchases when he gave me that serious "we are out of money" look. There was no more, and I knew that my Christmas shopping was not complete. I can still remember the tears I shed on that parking lot. Yes, I understand.

I am sure you have had similar times. Some of you may have just married and the hard times haven't yet come. The babies haven't started. One of the things we face if we marry a minister is that we will never be wealthy, in the coin of the realm. We don't consider ourselves wealthy, and we indulge in little pity parties from time to time. However, most of the world would look at you and me and conclude we are affluent people. Now I can give you a whole speech about the blessings of ministry, and the fringe benefits that accompany ministry, but they are not all on the first and the fifteenth of the month. I hope that you will not go through ministry resentful of that fact, but will learn to accept it. There are lots of blessings, but cash is not always one of them.

Ministers are paid better now than they used to be. I don't think there is any question about that. In fact, I can hardly conceive of some of the salaries that I hear for church staff positions. Things have changed a great deal, but I believe we know that we will never make a whole lot of money. That is just another reason for being good stewards of what we do have.

Even if you are not a minister's wife, chances are you experience financial difficulties from time to time. It can happen to anyone, but if you have your faith you should not resent these situations. Being an active member of your church will sustain you with its own blessings through good times and bad.

Money is one area where we all need goals. I had never had a financial goal until a couple of years ago. I once asked my husband, "What in the world would I have for a financial goal?" Long ago I had turned the finances over to him, admitting defeat. I had come to the realistic conclusion that I am not blessed with business acumen. I know he has spent many a sleepless night wondering what would happen to me if he died; I have spent a few of those myself. He says I would give it all to the kids in the first year! I really wouldn't do that, but I might give it to the grandchildren!

When you pray about what the Lord wants you to do, He *will* impress something on you. I got an impression like that, when I was fifty-five years old and Landrum was sixty. I don't even like to think about it, but most of the Leavell men died in their sixties or earlier. The culprit was usually high blood pressure, for which we now have medication, but anything can happen. I began to realize that I needed to know something about finances. One authority gave this startling statistic: "Of every one hundred people reaching sixty-five, only 2 percent are financially independent. Twenty-three have to continue to work and seventy-five are dependent on government, charity, friends or relatives."

With all due respect, Landrum has tried to educate me about money management. I wish I could tell you the number of times he has called me over to his desk and said, "I want to show you about this insurance." "I want you to know how to figure income tax." "This is where I keep important papers." It would be like a red flag before a bull. It would irritate me—I did not want to see it, I did not want to talk about it, I had absolutely zero interest. It wasn't that he had not tried, but I did not respond. I guess it had to be my idea. I had to come to the realization that financial goals are important.

About that same time Landrum was in revival with a good friend in the Dallas area. The friend and his second wife had only been married a short time, his first wife having died. The second wife had been a widow for ten years. She was forty-one years old at the time of her husband's death and knew very little about finances, but when she inherited his business, she really had to learn fast.

I asked her what she wanted to do in her new role as a preacher's wife, and she responded, "I would really like to talk to women about finances and what to do if they were left a widow." It was as if she was put there at that time for me. I told her what a contribution I thought that would be and that it would fill such a need. She was dubious because she said people don't like to talk about death, and she had a point. Most of us act as though it will never happen; I know I had ignored the possibility for fifty-five years. But it is important for us to learn everything we can about finances. This means going to seminars, reading everything in sight, and asking questions.

I remember saying to her, "I don't even know enough to ask questions." She said, "I didn't either, but even if you don't learn the meaning of but one term, it can help you." You will learn a little more the next time, and a little bit more the next. I can tell you I still know very little, but I know more than I did a couple of years ago. That's the rewarding part.

My first goal was to save $25 a week out of my grocery money, which would be about $1,000 in a year. When I got $1,000 I was going to invest it. I did not know *anything* about investing, but I knew that you only learn when you do something yourself. I decided I was going to take my $1,000 and invest it unassisted. I told

Landrum I did not want help from him or anyone else—I would do it myself! Some of you are so good at this you may not even be able to relate to my ignorance.

I called Clay Corvin, the seminary's vice-president for business affairs, and asked him to name me about five places to call for interest rates. I had learned what a CD was, and I knew that you bought those at the bank. I was going to find the best yield, invest my money, and sit back after taking my first feeble steps in money management!

I called the five places, and you can tell about how long ago this was by the interest rates. I remember calling one savings and loan in New Orleans. I tried to act intelligent, and asked, "Could you tell me what you are paying on CDs?" She said 9.4 and I thanked her. I called a bank nearby with the same question and the answer was 9.10. I called the others on my list and when Landrum came in, I told him I was going to put my money in the neighboring bank at 9.10. He said that was fine, but why? I told him about the figures I had gathered, and that the savings and loan was 9.4 and the bank was 9.10. Now doesn't everybody know that 10 is more than 4? He was speechless. He answered, "Honey, I don't care how many zeros you put after one, it is still one." Can you believe I was that dumb? I didn't know that 9.10 was less than 9.4.

Then Landrum said, "Before you have a fit, that probably didn't cost you over seventy cents." I said, "I don't care. It's the principle of the thing!" I thought I had been purposely tricked. My friend was right, I did learn something: 10 is not more than 4 when it follows a decimal point! I will *never* make that mistake again. I have so far to go, but I'm making progress. I know terms that I didn't know a few years ago, and the financial page is no longer just Greek to me.

Where you have the least interest is always where you need the most help. I had no interest in the financial realm, and that was where I needed the most help. So I set some concrete financial goals, and continue to set them. Let us examine now some important aspects of money management.

Wealth's Subtlety

Wealth is subtle. It is not always what it seems, and it affects us in subtle ways. Since stewardship is mandatory for Christian workers, it is important that these subtleties of wealth be understood. If we are not in a right relationship with our money, then we are not in a right relationship with God. These go together.

Let me hasten to tell you that in spite of my financial ignorance, I understood about the tithe. I always gave a tithe, even before I became Mrs. Landrum Leavell. I was not taught this at home, but somewhere along the line I became convicted and convinced about the necessity of tithing. I did not understand about spending the nine-tenths, but I always knew where God's tenth went: to the church. If we are not faithful in our stewardship to God, it affects our whole relationship with Him.

I have heard my husband use the example of a banker. You can't get right with your banker if you have a past due note, can you? If you owe somebody money, you cannot have good rapport with him. We owe God. The tithe is the rent we pay for the space we occupy on this earth, and if we use that money other than for what it was intended, our relationship with Him is not going to be all it ought to be.

Sixteen of the thirty-eight parables of Jesus are concerned with stewardship. There are more references to money than even to salvation in the Scriptures. Jesus dealt with money matters because *money matters*. Jesus knew that there was a subtlety connected with wealth, that the devil would get to us where money is concerned. You remember Satan's first attack against Job related to his finances.

I didn't know for a long time that there were preachers who don't tithe. I just thought that came with the territory. I have known staff people who were fired because the preacher or church leaders found out they were not tithers. Your influence will vanish if the church ever finds out that you are not honest with God when it comes to the tithe. To give little says much. Money absolutely matters.

Do you recall from Mark's gospel that Jesus sat over the treasury and watched? Do you remember the widow who gave her mite? He knows what we do with our money—we can't hide.

Money matters at home too. The truth is that 50 percent of divorces have to do with problems about money and money management. Somewhere I read that it is no longer "until death do we part" but "until debt do we part." We have huge arguments over finances, and those who fuss the most about money are in the middle-income bracket. When you are poor, there is no money left over. When you are rich, there is money to spend as one wishes. So the ones who really do the most arguing are the ones in middle-income positions.

When there are discretionary funds after the bills are paid, the problems begin. He wants to spend the amount one way, and she wants to spend it another. She wants a new dress; he thinks he has to have new fishing tackle. He wants a boat; she wants dining room furniture. This is an important subject. For ministers' wives in particular, time and money are the two primary problem areas in the marriage.

And when any family is in continuous discord over money or lack of it, it puts a tremendous strain on family relationships. A woman's financial management must be such that she earns the respect of her spouse and the other members of her church. We *must* learn to manage our wealth.

A major subtlety is the belief that money is a substitute for love. We can look at family after family in which husbands are devoting themselves to amassing wealth. One day they wake up to discover their families are hopelessly fragmented. During the sixties we saw a whole generation rebel against being indulged with material things, while at the same time being denied personal attention, affection, and love. Just remember that money is never a substitute for love.

Another subtlety of wealth is mentioned in Proverbs. In 23:4 we read, "Labor not to be rich," and the reason is given in 23:5: "for riches certainly make themselves wings. . . ." In other words money is temporal, and how foolish it is to make it the top priority of life. It can be here today and gone tomorrow. October 19, 1988, is the best example I know of that. People that were worth a great deal of money on October 18 found their net worth had declined significantly in one day. All riches really are unpredictable and fleeting.

The wisdom writers do not condemn wealth as such, but they condemn making wealth one's chief aim. Have you known people who made this error? I have a friend who claimed that her main goals in life were to be rich and to marry a rich man. Oh, the foolishness of making money our first love. Christ is not against men owning wealth. He is against wealth owning men. Proverbs 11:28 says, "He that trusteth in his riches shall fall: but the righteous shall flourish as a branch." Righteousness should be our chief aim, not money. If money comes, fine, but don't make it your number one goal.

Remember, children follow our example. If we want to teach proper values, we must remind them that money is a good servant but a jealous master.

Money has ruined many people. We have friends who have managed it beautifully and have other friends whom it has ruined. Until put to the test, we really can't say how we would handle wealth. The Scripture says, "The love of money is the root of all evil." Every one of us is vulnerable at this point.

As wives, we have to take responsibility for the influence that we have in this regard. I've seen numerous pushy and ambitious women contribute to the destruction of their family values. Does this describe you? If you are in doubt, ask yourself this question: if you stated your most important life goal, would it have to do with attaining prosperity, status, or financial security?

If wealth guarantees happiness, America should be the happiest nation in the world. Instead, we have an inordinately high rate of suicide. In the prosperous community of Hollywood, you will find some of the most married and divorced, the most immoral, the most miserable people on earth. What should this teach us? We must possess our possessions or they will possess us. We cannot let wealth subtly take over our lives.

Wealth Secured

How do we get this money? Does the Scripture have anything to say to us in this way?

Wealth dishonestly acquired brings sorrow. Proverbs 15:27 tells us, "He that is greedy of gain troubleth his own house." I am told that the word translated here as "gain" comes from one that means "cut." The person in this verse is the one who wants the shortcut in everything. This is the one who is greedy, in a hurry to get rich. He is willing to cheat on his income tax, or take bribes.

Anyone who has a greedy spirit gives the indication of a character flaw. As Jesus asked in Mark 8:36, "For what shall it profit a man, if he shall gain the whole world, and lose his own soul?" The implied answer is *nothing*. Let's remember that. We see people prosper who have gotten money dishonestly, but they won't prosper forever. We reap what we sow, and in God's own time, He will take care of these matters. "Vengeance is truly mine, saith the Lord."

The money we do earn should be acquired by honest means, but we must still avoid get-rich-quick schemes. The writer of Proverbs told us in Proverbs 13:11, "Wealth gotten by vanity shall be diminished: but he that gathereth by labour shall increase." In other words, wealth hastily gotten will dwindle, but he that gathers *little by little* increases it. My $25 a week was little by little, but at the end of the year I had $1,000. I don't know about you, but that is big money to me. We are better able to handle it when it comes a little at a time.

There is something different about people who inherit money. Many times they act foolish because they don't know what to do with it. When we lived in Texas, someone said that there was more second generation wealth in our town than you could imagine. But young people who did not earn it or work for it seldom know how to handle money—they have "too much too soon." And get-rich-quick schemes without corresponding work undermine character. Remember that when it comes to your children. I don't believe in giving children a lot of money; they need to learn for themselves the value of a dollar.

In Proverbs 28:20 it states, "A faithful man shall abound with blessings; but he that maketh haste to be rich shall not be innocent." In a sense we are all tempted by get-rich-quick schemes, and if you have not, you will be. When we first came to the seminary, one of our friends invited us to hear a man who was seeking investors for a silver mine in Mexico. We were new on campus and accepted all invitations, so we went and listened. We didn't have any money to invest, but if we had, I would like to think that we were smarter than that friend, whom we understand invested $30,000. Those schemes are too good to be true. Sure enough, *all* the investors lost their money.

In Howard L. Dayton, Jr.'s *Getting Out of Debt*, eight rules are listed for judging if an offer is a sound investment or not:

1) Is the prospect of a large profit "practically guaranteed"?

2) Does the decision to invest need to be made quickly, allowing you no opportunity to thoroughly investigate the investment or the promoter?

3) Does the promoter say he has an "excellent track record," and is doing you a "favor" by allowing you to invest with him? [That is a common line that is not necessarily true.]

4) Does the investment offer attractive tax deductions as an incentive?

5) Do you know little or nothing about the particular investment?

6) Is very little said about the risk of losing money?

7) Does the investment appear to require no effort on your part?

8) Are you promised a "handsome profit" quickly?

Any time you encounter one or more danger signals, remember Mrs. Leavell told you to go *slow*.

The way we need to secure our money is through plain ole hard *work*. James 1:25 says, ". . . but a doer of the work, this man shall be blessed in his deed." Work is not a dirty word. In fact, I am very grateful for it. I don't know where I got my love for work, but I have it and I'm thankful.

I heard Mary Crowley say how much she enjoyed her work and express amazement that they actually paid her for it. A person who is in God's will feels this way. If you are a minister's wife, a paycheck is like a fringe benefit. You should love your work enough to do it whether or not you get paid.

I don't want a preacher who only does what he does because he is paid for it. It should be done out of love for the Lord. I like to think my service for the Lord is not done just because I am a preacher's wife. If we love the Lord, if He has gifted us, we will find a place of service and enjoy serving, and this goes for all Christian women. Do you remember the song "Living for Jesus"? We don't sing it too much anymore. "Living for Jesus . . . striving to please Him in all that I do."

The Bible says, "If you work for the thing you believe in you are rich, though the way is rough." If we are working only for money, we can never make enough. If we are working because we love it, then we will find fulfillment and peace.

The old Protestant "work ethic" seems to be missing today. That is the reason we are discovering that Japanese cars are often made better than American ones. Many imported goods are more popular than American ones because of their good quality. We don't have pride in workmanship anymore—we are more interested in time off and fringe benefits. Talk with pulpit committees and they will tell you how frequently they have encountered this attitude. It seems many preachers and their wives are not nearly as concerned about their contribution as they are about the benefits. Whatever happened to concern for doing the will of God at any cost? All through Scripture, laziness and idleness are discouraged. We are told an idle mind is the devil's workshop.

The ministry is work. When Landrum talks on church growth, he always reminds people that the ministry is not a forty-hour week. When you see churches that grow, and effective preachers, you can well know that they have paid the price in work. My husband also says there are two things a church will fire you for: one is being lazy and the other is being immoral. If you work and stay clean morally, I don't believe many churches will run you off.

I agree with Jim Henry, who said that he believed it took longer for neglect to catch up with you in the ministry than anywhere, but when your laziness is discovered you will go down quicker than anywhere. When it does catch up with you, it is going to happen so quickly you won't have time to say grace over it.

Let's be workers. If you don't set new goals, if you don't learn and set some standards for yourself, life will get monotonous. We all need the fresh enthusiasm that comes when we *do* something, if we just get busy and work.

The Bible has told us the answer to the question of securing wealth. It must be earned slowly through honest work, and not acquired quickly in great amounts. And work has its own rewards: it challenges your mind, makes productive use of your time, helps others, and, in the ministry, allows you to demonstrate your devotion to God.

Wealth Spent

It matters how Christians secure their money, but it is likewise important how they spend it. We have already mentioned the need to put God first. I trust you take God's tithe off the top. Ministers' wives in particular must practice tithing before preaching it: to others. In Proverbs, Exodus, and Malachi we are given instructions concerning money. We know what the Scripture has to say about it: when a man puts money first, he usually puts God last.

I read that "an effective way of helping visualize God's involvement in your giving is to imagine you are placing your gift in the nailed scarred hands of Jesus." I thought that was excellent. We give through the church, but we are really giving it to Him, to be used in His work. Why? Simply because He told us to—"if you love me, mind me" (keep My commandments).

Proverbs 3:9-10 says, "Honour the Lord with thy substance, and with the first fruits of all thine increase: So shall thy barns be filled with plenty, and thy presses shall burst out with new wine." That doesn't mean if we do this we will escape all misfortunes. Worldly goods are not a guarantee of heavenly acceptance or an indication of God's blessings. Tithing is practiced to demonstrate obedience to God, not to win favor.

The Scripture says that He blesses faithful tithers, but it does not always mean financial blessing. There are many kinds of blessings. The Bible often speaks of trouble. We are not promised escape from problems because we are faithful, but we are going to have the assurance that we are doing what the Lord wants us to do. There are spiritual rewards and sometimes material rewards. We will not always escape normal problems that occur to all of us in life, so the mark of a successful Christian is his or her faithfulness.

I can't say I have all the faith I should. I can't say I pray all I should, or read my Bible all I should. But I can say I am faithful in tithing. This is one tangible way we can measure our faithfulness.

I believe that it is impossible to continue violating a scriptural principle without suffering the consequences. We may get along for awhile, but eventually we'll reap what we have sown. You may not agree with my theology, but I believe the Lord collects His tithe. I have seen it. If we are faithful we never have to wonder if our problems are the result of unfaithfulness. We can always know we have been honest with God and have put Him first.

In 1 Corinthians 16 we are told how to tithe. We are reminded in 1 Corinthians 16:2 to be regular in giving on the first day of the week. Some of us get paid every two weeks. I know people who divide the tithe to establish a regular weekly pattern. My mother-in-law, I know, wrote a check for her tithe, but she always put something in the offering plate as it went by. She had very little but I can remember many a night in our church when she was visiting that she would put a quarter in as an act of worship. The Scripture admonishes us to give regularly.

Every one of you "lay by him in store as God has prospered." Giving needs to be systematic and it needs to be proportionate, "that there be no gatherings when I come." The best way to be a tither and stay faithful is never to get behind. Like anything else, it is hard to catch up.

The one time in our married life when Landrum and I were tempted to get behind was during his seminary days. We were driving 700 miles a week to our church in north Mississippi, 350 miles each way and that was back before we had interstate highways. Landrum is one of these who likes to have emergency money, and one time, after he was paid at the Mississippi church, he said, "Honey, I don't think I will put any tithe in Sunday. I'll take it with me just in case we need it, and put it in next Sunday." I knew I didn't want to go back to New Orleans with God's tithe in my pocket. I replied, "No. I'd rather put it in and take our chances."

If we are human, occasionally we think of what we could do with all that money. I remember some friends inviting us to go to a New Orleans Saints exhibition football game. We were to meet them at the Superdome on Saturday night. While we were waiting upstairs for our friends, I kept watching the people as they went in. Families with three and four children went in with popcorn, beer, soda, or food of some kind. I was calculating all this in my mind. When we sat down with our friends, I said, "I don't see how they do it. I don't see how they buy tickets, pay to park, and buy snacks for several kids." She said, "Jo Ann, I know. They don't tithe!" It struck me as funny, but she was right—they don't tithe. Yes, there are many ways you could spend God's 10 percent, but there is only one way to be faithful.

Wealth Strategies

Tithing is the first way you should spend your money, but then

your debts need attention. Failure to pay your personal bills regularly has its consequences, such as poor credit ratings. My father,
who was a banker, felt this could be a serious indictment against the
ministry especially. He helped many a minister get his finances in
order over the years. In Proverbs 22:7 it says, "The rich ruleth over
the poor, and the borrower is servant to the lender." We are servants
when we are in debt. We are told that the average American spends
$400 a year more than he earns. Expenses will always tend to rise
higher than income. You know the old "too much month at the end
of the money" story. It is true for you and me.

I remember one time my sister got a raise and I was rejoicing with
her. I told her, "Oh, that is wonderful." She said, "I don't know, Jo
Ann. It will just mean we have a little bit more before we are broke!"
Isn't that the way it is? We get a fifty-dollar raise and our wants
increase fifty dollars a month or more.

Are you in debt? If you are unable to pay an entire bill when it
comes, if you carry any balance, you are a member of the debt set.
The goal is to rid yourself of debt, but if you can't do it on your own,
by all means seek help There are many qualified church members
willing to help you get your finances in order.

Another way we can know we are in debt is this. Does the amount
owed on an item exceed its current asset value? Think about your
car, for instance. When you drove your car out of the showroom,
you probably could not sell it the next day and pay off the note. The
cash proceeds would not be enough to cover the amount owed, and
this is true with any depreciating asset. Take furniture. Buy furniture one day and you couldn't get your money out of it the next day.

Most of us are in debt. Ideally they say a house is the only thing
you ought to go into debt to buy. We never were able to pay cash for
a car. Maybe we did not work at it hard enough. I am told that in five
to eight years, if you wanted to, you could be in a financial position
to pay cash. Money must be managed to avoid debt, so let's look at
some wealth strategies.

The way to manage money is to establish a written budget. What
will your written budget do?

1) It sets guidelines. You ask yourself what expenses are necessary
and what expenses can be reduced or eliminated. We have gotten
totally confused about the difference between needs and wants.

Our needs are minimal. Our appetite is whetted, however, so that we just keep wanting and wanting. I read this encouraging statement: "Anybody who can write down figures can find a way out of their financial problems." If you will write down a budget and stick to it, I don't care what your problems are, you can work out of them. A budget is a plan for spending.

2) It also helps you analyze patterns, some that are likely not good patterns. Some people have even suggested a method of tracking our dollars before setting a budget. This could be done if everyone who spends part of the income would write down every expenditure for a month. These expenses would then be compiled in columns for insurance, food, clothing, eating out, bills—*everything*. Then we can make adjustments, cut out the fat, and develop a budget in keeping with the needs of the family. You probably would be amazed at how much money "gets away" in frivolous ways.

One of our favorite pastimes in New Orleans is going to Morning Call for coffee and/or beignets. Landrum and I started recording our expenses, and it is incredible how much our little "coffee breaks" were costing. Try writing down your expenditures—it may help you change some of your spending habits and get a handle on your money.

3) It introduces an attitude of control by discouraging impulse buying. There is not a one of us who is not guilty of such buying. In fact, they say that 70 percent of all goods are bought on impulse. That is a fantastic percentage. When you have a written budget, you no longer operate on impulse. Someone suggested, "If you want to buy something, put it on an impulse list, wait thirty days, and pray about it. Then decide if you really need it."

Another suggestion is, never carry more than five dollars in cash with you—no credit cards or checks. Leave the rest of your money at home. If you find something you want, go home and get the money. That will give you time to think about it, and you will have avoided impulse buying. I'm told this will increase your spendable income by about 20 percent. Is that worth the inconvenience? You bet!

4) Budgets help eliminate marital conflict and create a closeness in the family. Money management becomes a team effort when you and your husband communicate about the budget. This kind of

planning requires the cooperation of both spouses. If you have older children, it involves their cooperation as well. Teenage children won't resent limitations nearly as much if you explain to them what you are doing and why you are doing it. They will rise to the occasion most of the time.

It is perfectly normal for children to want the name-brand articles. But the Scripture says that part of our teaching responsibility is not to encourage conformity to this world. Years of affirmation, praise for positive action, and unconditional love can prepare children best for the denial of material things. This love is expressed best by eye contact, physical contact, focused attention, and loving discipline. If we provide these at home, when the time comes to say "no" or "you can't have that," it will be accepted better than if we had not opened these lines of communication.

Following your budget is the first step in preventing debt, but how do you begin repaying what you do owe? Make a list of all assets, that is, everything you own of material value. It will probably surprise you. We have more than we think. Then make a list of all debts, that is, everything you owe. If you are trying to get out of debt, pay off those that have the highest interest rate first. Establish a repayment schedule; it will give you a sense of accomplishment, and the incentive to persist in your plan. You might wish to send a copy of your repayment plan to your creditors. If they know you are trying, that you have a repayment schedule, they are going to be patient with you.

My mother-in-law could not always pay. She lived her last years basically on social security, and with help the family gave her. Sometimes she could not pay a bill in its entirety, but she would pay something on it every month. She would let people know she was working at it. I don't know anyone who won't go along with that sort of determination.

Here is another management strategy: apply additional income to greatest needs. Ministers often receive extra income from performing weddings, leading revivals, and sometimes just getting gifts from generous church members. Budget first on the basis of your known income. Then if you earn overtime, if you receive an income tax refund, if you have a revival, if you have an odd job or any other income, put it in its entirety, after tithe, on a debt.

We don't ordinarily do this. What happens when we get an income tax refund? We think of throwing a party, or buying something. We never think of applying that money to our debts or savings. Why not? If we did, we would be in a lot better financial condition.

In order to make a budget work, you must be careful to accumulate no new debts. Of course, a foolproof way is to pay cash. Beware of plastic money. I recall someone having said, "We ought to put all our credit cards on a cookie sheet. Put them in a 350 degree oven, and leave it for twenty minutes. Then they would all be ruined." We all want a good credit rating, and you get that by paying bills. When bills become a problem, easy credit is often the culprit. Use credit cards for a few purchases here and there, as a convenience, to defer payments, or to build a good credit record, but the smart way to use them is *not* to use them.

Be content with what you have. Paul admonished us to be content in whatever state we find ourselves. If he could be content in jail, he could be that way wherever he was. Most of us are not that content, and one prime reason is advertising's main goal of creating discontent. Many Americans watch fifty to one hundred television commercials a day. Those commercials are trying to accomplish one thing, and that is to make the viewers buy something. But coveting is to be avoided at all costs.

Contentment is a virtue in life we ought to develop. It is the opposite of greed, and keeps us within our budgets. Are you learning to be content? Affluence has ruined many a man, even many a Baptist preacher. The desire for money can lead to misplaced priorities, and the end result of that, according to Scripture, is "they have wandered away from the faith." This love of money is a sin that gives birth to many other sins and will lead to a person's financial bind. Remember wealth's subtlety and don't let it dull your spiritual sensitivity.

Wealth Saved

After we have developed a budget and some debt-paying strategies, we hope to have some funds left over to save! But first we must break the "spending syndrome." As someone commented, "Being financially secure doesn't take brilliance or luck—just discipline."

It takes real discipline to put away part of what you earn.

I've always heard a good plan is to tithe 10 percent and save 10 percent. When our children were growing up, Landrum and I tried to get them to practice saving, and it is something we continue to practice. If saving 10 percent seems unrealistic right now, try 5 percent. The important thing is regular discipline.

The place to begin saving, for most of us, is to *pay off our debts.* I've read that "the best way to earn 18 percent, risk free, tax-free, is not to have to pay it on a credit card loan. The best way to earn 12 percent is not to have to pay it on an auto loan. What could be simpler or more effective?" Stop charging, stop instant gratification, because the resulting interest eats into your savings. If you want to buy something, save up for it.

I read of a wonderful way to train children in how to spend a dollar, and it was done with five empty peanut butter jars. These were labeled tithe, taxes, savings to spend, savings to invest, and discretionary. The dollar was exchanged for ten dimes, and distributed as follows—one dime for tithe, two dimes in taxes, one dime to save to spend for vacations or some special item, one dime to invest for retirement, and five dimes in the one marked discretionary to spend for anything desired. This is teaching a child to operate on 60 percent of his income, plus it teaches the invaluable lessons of tithing and saving.

I think the reason I was so impressed with that plan is because it resembled one of my own when our children were small. Money was extremely tight, and Landrum gave me a weekly check to manage the house and the children's needs. I always had a false sense of wealth when I got that check, and was penniless before the week was over. I woke up one day to the fact that most of that money was already committed. I got baby food jars, and began distributing the money as soon as my check was cashed. They were labeled tithe, groceries, allowances, beauty shop, etc., and it made all the difference in the world. The children learned early to go straight to the proper jar for their needs, and it was *wonderful* when Friday came for the beauty shop and the money was there!

I suggest you need at least three jars if you are going to put your finances in perspective.

1) Pay God.

2) Pay yourself (savings).

3) Pay your bills.

Good stewardship in these three areas will result in financial success.

Wealth Shared

What would you say is the difference between having money and being materialistic? You shouldn't feel bad if you earn money by doing something worthwhile, but you should worry if it is all spent selfishly. If all we think about is buying a bigger house or another car, that's materialism. If your pockets are full, and your hearts empty, that also is materialism.

Let me hasten to add that the materialistic spirit has little to do with the amount of money earned. I've heard it said that a dime over the eye can impair your vision as much as a dollar.

Maybe you say that you don't live close to any "misery villages," that you don't know anybody hungry. Believe me, there are pockets of need all around you. In Wichita Falls our church always gave away Christmas baskets to the needy. They were delivered by our deacons, who would come back wide-eyed from their firsthand view of poverty and human need. This type of thing must be done by deliberate action because most of us are not going to stumble on those with "real" problems. I heard a missionary nurse say that even on the mission field the people with severe needs were not those clamoring for your attention when you docked but those hidden away in huts waiting for someone with compassion.

I received a call before Easter once from a longtime friend. He said, "Do you know any student on your campus who may not have a new Easter outfit?" "Of course," I replied, and I had the privilege of outfitting a lovely young woman. She was thrilled, and I rejoiced at being a part of the incredible generosity of my friend.

What about you? Do the needs of the world, the hurts of people, cry so loud that it seems as if someone were calling your name? Give before the impulse cools off or goes away. No matter how limited your ability there are ways to get involved.

Maybe you think only of yourself and your family rather than being genuinely interested in the needs of others. When was the last time you gave money to someone else that you could have spent selfishly? Every dollar that comes your way comes for a purpose. At least part of it should be spent to make the world a better place. Money is not the only way to share, but it may be a good place to begin.

Money brings with it some hidden pitfalls, and even a minister's wife is not immune to them. We must all pay attention to how we manage our money. It involves tithing, following a budget, paying off debts, putting away savings—and don't neglect to share when you can!

PART IV

Reaffirmation of the Future

CHAPTER 13

LOOK FORWARD:
Pursuing Our Goals

LIFE CAN BE BEST UNDERSTOOD by looking backward, looking within, and looking around, as we have been doing. However, it must be lived by looking forward. Setting goals and pursuing them leads us all to realizing our God-given potential.

I listened to a series of tapes once which prompted me to put my goals on paper. The tapes said we need goals in six areas of our lives: spiritual, mental, physical, family, social, and financial. That pretty well covers everything, doesn't it? If you have a goal in all six areas, you'll have a well-balanced life. In a sense, all six are spiritual goals for the Christian. A goal is simply a target for our behavior and is said to be the common link among high achievers. You choose a goal, and then that choice controls you.

What is the difference between a goal and a desire? A goal is something I want which I can control. A desire is something I want, but I cannot control. A wish is a desire without any subsequent effort.

Let me illustrate the difference. I want my husband to lose weight. This is a desire, because I can't control it. I cannot actually do anything to make him lose weight.

What if I want to lose weight? That's a goal. I am the only one who has control over what goes in my mouth. What about this one? I want a godly marriage. A godly marriage is really a desire because I don't have full control over this. A better goal would be, I want to be a godly wife. That's something over which I have control.

Landrum and I have always talked about things we wanted for our home and our children, but up until a few years ago I had never written my goals on paper. It revolutionized my life to put them in writing, because it clarifies them. You get them where you can see them, and it makes you determined to think through every area of your life. Remember that Jesus had goals. The Scripture says, "He set His face toward Jerusalem." What did He say from the cross? "It is finished." He set goals and accomplished what He set out to do.

Of those six areas I named, where do you have the least interest? That is a foolproof way to determine your greatest area of need. Are you satisfied with yourself? What is Jesus doing in your life today? Where are you going? If you are average, only 10 percent of you readers could tell me. Just 3 percent have ever put goals on paper. Ask yourself, "What is the best use of my time *now*, so I can be where I want in ten years?"

I have heard the future referred to as the "yet to be." It is out there for all of us, and we want to make it as good as we possibly can. If I had one bit of advice to give, it would be to embark consciously on a positive course of action. Take charge of your life. It is never too late.

Don't keep postponing. If you are in a paralyzed state, it is *your* decision to get out of it and no one can do it for you. Dissatisfaction with one's self often precedes growth. Most people would rather stagnate than change direction, but don't be content to be "average." Get angry with mediocrity. Success is learning to be your *best*.

Decide to Grow

If you pursue goals, it will require three things: a decision, discipline, and determination. You decide you want to grow and choose a goal. Discipline and determination must follow to make it happen. Now let's look at this decision.

Start simply. Don't jump in there and have fourteen goals—begin with one area. Goals should stretch you, not break you. Make yourself do what is necessary to grow in one of these areas. Weaknesses are not going to be changed overnight, but they can be changed by deliberate effort.

Take some definite steps. Visualize the person you want to be; form mental pictures of your future. Goals have been called "internalized dreams," and the steps necessary to accomplish these dreams are called plans and objectives. Make a list of what must be done to achieve your goal and say "no" to anything that is not going to help get you there. Every time you take a new growth step, the next one seems easier and more possible to achieve. Take responsibility for your own actions. Challenge yourself.

One of the questions I asked my class on a test was, if you had to grade yourself spiritually, from one to ten with ten being the highest, what would you say your spiritual temperature is? The students were honest, answering anywhere from three to eight. But your spiritual walk with the Lord is something *you* can control. Faithfulness in the spiritual realm will help us live by the peace of God rather than the pressures of life.

Do you have a mental goal? Unless you try something beyond what you have already mastered, you will never grow. I can talk a long time on this, because it's one of my problem areas. Landrum used to tell people, which I resented highly, that if it wasn't in *Reader's Digest*, don't ask Jo Ann, for she wouldn't know. That was true, because from the time I got out of college, I didn't read much. I decided this was an area in which I needed to grow, and I'm convinced the Lord has given me a new love for study. How long has it been since you've read a book? I'm told only 23 percent of the Christian public ever reads a book. Eighty percent of these are women.

Some of you may be reluctant to set a goal of reading more because you worry you won't have the time. But you can read during your "I" time, which I discussed in the time management chapter. There are lots of ways to slip more reading time into your busy life. Take books with you in the car or to the doctor's office. Keep good reading material strategically located in your home—by the bed, in the bathroom, and by your favorite chair—or listen to informative tapes. If this is a goal in the mental area of your life, you must decide to use your time for study.

One of our faculty members was about fifty when she was deciding whether or not to go back to school and get her doctorate. She was discussing it with her father, and told him, "In five years I'm going to be fifty-five." Her wise father looked at her and said, "How old will you be in five years if you don't go back?" She later came to teach at the seminary. Time is marching on.

I have another friend who is a high school graduate. She says many is the time she drove up to the university, parked her car in front, but never worked up her nerve to go in. How sad! We must understand that the mental area in our lives needs attention, and it's never too late to start.

One of my goals several years ago was to take a class at the seminary. Now before you think that sounded easy, I was literally scared to death. I had not been in a classroom in thirty-five years. I wasn't sure my brain still worked! Apprehension increased when I thought, "Oh my soul, what if I embarrass the president!" I had a lot at stake. At first I thought I would just audit, but I knew myself well enough to know that if I audited, I wouldn't give it my best effort. Sooo, I decided to jump in there, take a course for credit, and let the chips fall where they may. I did it, and I felt good about myself. I decided to set a goal and met it even though it was difficult.

Landrum had a man in his evangelism class who was eighty. When asked why he wanted to take evangelism, he answered, "I always wanted to do a better job of talking to people about the Lord." Isn't it exciting to know people who are still interested in growing? It reminds me of this statement: "You are young and useful at any age if you are still planning for tomorrow." Another says, "If what you did yesterday seems big and important, then you haven't done anything today."

My mother-in-law took typing at the YMCA when she was eighty-two. Her dream was to write a book, and learning to type would contribute to that goal. She practiced on letters to her family. I might add—she finished the book!

My mental goal at the moment is this book. When I was deliberating and agonizing over whether or not I could do this, I read, "If you are not stretching yourself and your talents, why not?" Good question. Well, believe me, it has been a stretching experience. I am *not* a writer. I told the Lord that over and over in my prayer time and tried every way to get out of it. At the risk of sounding pious, I simply felt a strong impression that this is what He wanted me to do. Landrum always says, if you can't forget these impressions, you'd better do something about them.

What about a physical goal? If we want to be in physical shape, we must have some physical goals of exercise and diet. Reaching such a goal is not going to happen overnight. A friend of mine decided about a year ago the physical side of her life was the one thing that was not under control. She has lost over fifty pounds and looks *wonderful.* It *can* happen.

Every year before I teach my class, my husband and I have this little game we play. I'll say, "Honey, what do you want me to tell them?" And then he responds exactly as I know he will, saying, "Tell them not to let themselves go." So, girls, don't let yourselves go! Guys, don't let yourselves go either! This is one of the worst things that happens to us when we settle into married life. We don't keep up our physical fitness. Ask God to give you a real interest in looking right.

What about family goals? Quality time with your family is the Lord's work. Have you set aside time for them?

Now that my children are grown, I made a commitment several years ago to write each of them a monthly letter including a calendar of our whereabouts. Landrum and I travel a great deal, and I want my children always to be able to find me if I'm needed. The monthly letters and calendars sounded like an easy goal when I wrote it down, but believe me, it has taken a great deal of "stick-to-itiveness" to pull it off.

Setting aside time for your children is a good family goal, but remember to set some goals for your role as a wife too. It's such a shame when the children leave the nest and the parents discover they have been growing apart from each other all these years. Even if you are currently busy raising your children, lay the groundwork now for a solid marriage after they're gone. The family area in our lives could always use some goals of improvement. Make that decision to grow.

Landrum and I sat down some time ago and made some "couple" goals. You need both individual and joint goals. Any growth goals requiring much change are going to need a lot of support from your loved ones. Establish your direction and then move toward mutually determined goals for your marriage and family.

The social area is not where I need a whole lot of help. I need some, but I am such a social being that I would spend all my time here. However, some of you need to set a goal for play—those things that add zest, fun, joy, and delight to life. Don't piously say, "I don't have time." Everyone, especially the pastor and his wife, occasionally needs to have some social life apart from the church and the children. This is good advice:

> When you play, play hard;
> When you work, don't play at all!

If you're uncomfortable in a social setting, that's the area which needs attention. Don't nurse your insecurity in the matter of social graces. Become assertive and do something to become more socially skilled. Try something new, like having some friends in your home for a meal every two weeks. If you did that, your insecurity would soon vanish. Say hello to three people you don't know; ask one stranger a day for the time. Plan some opportunities to be more socially active.

Remember this: where you have the least interest is where you need the most help. I have absolutely zero interest in the financial realm, which I have already shared with you. Because of my lack of interest, I continue to make financial goals my number one priority.

My latest financial goal is to save the same twenty-five dollars a week I have been investing, and give it away. I can never tell you what a joy this has been. I give most of it anonymously, but I have received great soul satisfaction in helping others.

The Koreans have a great custom you may want to adopt. They give a "thanks offering" to the Lord every time something good happens to them. If they have a baby, get a raise, or in any other way experience God's blessings, they respond with a gift of gratitude.

Where do you have the least interest? Recognize areas of weakness and seek to overcome them. Pray about what you think the Lord wants you to do and move in that direction. Take it slow and start where you will have reasonably sure success. If your physical goal is to lose fifty pounds, start with ten. Achieve that goal and go for ten pounds more. Success will give you the motivation to continue.

We have a friend who is on a church staff. She went on a liquid diet under a doctor's care and lost 110 pounds. "I gave myself nine months," she said. "You can make a baby in nine months. I'll make a new person in nine months." She decided on a time limit.

Let's take this goal setting a step at a time. Give yourself one goal a day and accomplish it, whatever else you have to drop. Unless we do some of these things, our lives are going to stay out of control.

My husband was interim pastor of a church which had not reached its Lottie Moon goal in five years. He insisted they go back and make the goal low enough so the people could reach it. This success gave them a sense of accomplishment. In just a short time they were back over the original amount. There is something defeating about goals that are not realistic. Go slow, decide on realistic goals, and you will find each small success builds confidence.

Be decisive because indecision eats up time.Learning to say "no" is a mark of Christian maturity. Say "no" to everything that would get you off course. You must *not* let people give you "jobs." Being asked is not synonymous with the Lord's will. You take them in keeping with the way you feel you are gifted. Look that person in the eye, smile, and say, "This is not what I do best."

Don't say "no" to everything. Determine what you do enjoy and do it. If you are undecided, just say, "Let me think about it." That buys you time to talk to the Lord and your husband. If it doesn't fit in with your goals and your gifts, forget it. You might offer to help them find somebody for the job.

Accept the fact that some people in your churches, and maybe even in your family, won't understand your choices. Avoid the temptation to be molded by your congregation or its pastor. God made each of us with widely varied needs, energies, goals, and ambitions. Remember: you do not owe anybody else an explanation for *your* priorities. Be kind but firm.

I've gotten very philosophical about the inevitability of criticism. I have concluded if others are talking about me, they are letting somebody else rest! They say that in ministry we need to develop a "calculated deafness." I concur with that statement. All of us could take a lesson from the weather. It pays no attention to criticism.

No matter how pure your motives, or how beautiful the completed project, there will be criticism. This is when you must look to the Lord for affirmation. Once I was involved in remodeling a seminary building and encountered some criticism over it. During one of my lowest moments I read this assurance from Scripture: "Let us not be weary in well doing: for in due season we shall reap, if we faint not" (Galatians 6:9).

I'm not suggesting criticism is never justified. In fact, the first thing I normally suggest is to ask yourself if the criticism has any merit. We can often learn and grow as a result of criticisms accepted, producing change.

If complaints persist, a talk with the critic may be in order. Keep in mind some of the most unlovable people in your congregation may simply need some attention and love from you.

Have you reached a plateau as a person? Don't be addicted to business as usual. Vary the order in which you do things. Anxiety is often connected with new situations and to avoid anxiety, we stay in dull routines. Being bumped out of a comfortable rut can be scary. I experienced anxiety when I signed up for my seminary course, and when I joined a weight-loss group. You will have anxiety the first time you participate in a Bible study group that requires preparation. Those are anxious moments. It is easier to stay in routines and not grow, but make a decision to do it. No one needs any encouragement to be average. By our choices, we determine what we are.

Discipline Yourself

If we live up to our God-given potential, it is going to require *discipline*. I know that is a dirty word. Pick out where you have the least interest, and then discipline yourself. The limitations you are willing to place on yourself determine your success. Growth requires effort, and it is going to cost you to work toward a goal. Do I need to remind you it will cost you more if you don't?

I'm told that by our mid-thirties we seldom learn anything new. I don't know about you, but I don't want to stagnate at any age. Goals are achieved only by deliberate effort and any worthwhile project takes *time*. Greatness is built from blocks of daily faithfulness to the task at hand. No achievement is accidental and skill comes only with practice. Most of us like the fruit of personal development, but few of us appreciate the pain of process.

Beginning anything new is going to cause pain. If you begin physical exercise, it will absolutely use muscles you didn't know you had, and you'll be sore. We have more evidence of pain with the physical area of life, but it's painful with the mental and spiritual also.

The disciplines of life get you where you want to go. Our instant society doesn't relish discomfort or inconveniences, yet we can't grow as Christians without these. Take the risk. You will never stub your toe standing still, but you will never get anywhere either. But you say, "I am afraid." You are abnormal if you aren't, but without risk you won't make much progress. Accept the possibility of setbacks. That doesn't mean we quit; we just have to come at it in a different way.

My son-in-law took the G.R.E., the Graduate Record Exam required for the Th.D. program, *eight* times. He didn't have the background in math, English, and other things he needed. The required score at that time was 950, and he only scored 760 his first try. In my mind, I just knew he would never make it.

I don't believe that ever occurred to Finis. You have to pay a fee every time you take it, and although he and Ann didn't have two dimes to rub together, he took the test two more times and was still in the 700s. Then he heard about a course which prepares people to pass the G.R.E. for a $300 fee. He took the course, and drove in to New Orleans from Baton Rouge one night every week for eight weeks. Talk about discipline! He took the G.R.E. again and made 910, and continued to take it until he passed! I don't know many people that disciplined in achieving something they want, but this is what it takes once you've made that decision.

Determination

Determination and perseverance pays off. Finis proved the wisdom of Helen Keller's statement, "We can do anything we want to do if we stick to it long enough." Hard work and long hours characterize most worthwhile projects.

Dwell on these statements I have heard or read:

About the only thing that comes without effort is old age!!
The only time success comes before work is in the dictionary.

> The difference between ordinary and extraordinary is that little extra.
> Give your best and then some.
> The person who gets ahead is the one who does more than is necessary and keeps on doing it.

I had one student wife say, "I want to do what Mrs. Leavell does," meaning speaking, traveling, and teaching. What she failed to understand is how many *years* I stayed home raising my children, being faithful to my church, persevering before I saw *any* spiritual growth worth speaking about. You see, nothing can happen *through* us that has not happened *to* us. We cannot teach unfelt truth. The Lord often tutors us privately before He chooses to use us publicly.

I heard Zig Ziglar say he gave hundreds of speeches before he was ever paid for one. He was determined.

Changes come slowly. Defining our purpose is a process that continues all through life. We must constantly shift and change, intentionally shaping our lives to the will of God and His call upon us.

Your life will not automatically stay under control. I wish it was something we could fix once and for all, but it's not. This must be reaffirmed every day you live. Your priorities will get out of sync. You will be negligent, especially in the areas where you are weakest. I could easily slip back and never make another decision financially, except to spend money. I know how to do that, but I will have to continue to set and follow goals in that area.

We live in an instant society and fool ourselves into expecting instant weight loss, instant maturity, instant success. These won't come instantaneously, but they *will* come if we plan a course of deliberate action. That plan includes: 1) a decision—keep it simple, in one area first; 2) discipline—success comes by "aspiration, inspiration, and perspiration"; and 3) the determination to stay with it. Challenge yourself, strain those muscles, choose a top priority, and don't quit. Remember "the establishment of a goal is the key to successful living." Commit to growth, commit to goals, and commit *all* to Jesus lest you *miss the blessing.*

CHAPTER 14

LOOK FORWARD:

Blessings

MINISTERS' WIVES, THIS CHAPTER is devoted completely to you. Let me start with this question. Have you ever known anybody who really *wanted* to be a preacher's wife?

I had not when I met and married a minister. I think we do young people an injustice when we talk about "fighting the call to preach." Somehow it leaves a bad taste in their mouths. It did in mine. I did not grow up around preachers.

I really am indebted to my mother-in-law, who was also a pastor's wife. She was a satisfied customer in ministry, and that rubbed off on me. She was a wonderful Christian lady and had a positive attitude toward being a pastor's wife. I love my role, and she deserves much of the credit because of the things she taught me about ministry.

I don't want you to come as close as I did to missing the blessing. Remember my request to tell the pulpit committees I was not a second staff member for the price of one? I am not real proud of that, but that was my attitude. I thought in ministry you did just as little as you could get by with. It wasn't that I didn't love the Lord. I don't know why I was so reluctant to serve Him, except I had been influenced to believe that no one in her right mind wanted to be in this position.

Perhaps you have experienced some of this negative input in your life. If you have never heard it before, I want to tell you the ministry can be *fun*. One minister's wife said, "There is nothing as exciting as living in a parsonage." Statistics reveal 80 percent of ministers and their wives are satisfied. I think that is pretty good. When you talk to ministers' wives or ministers who are unhappy in their roles, keep it in perspective. Realize they make up a small 20 percent, and 80 percent are comfortable and happy to be in the clergy. I hope you are one of those.

My attitude has so significantly changed that I really feel sorry for those who don't have the privilege of being a minister's wife. I feel now this is the grandest thing that can happen to anybody.

We moved to the seminary when our daughter was in her senior year of high school. I was trying to think of everything positive I could tell her. I said, "Honey, who knows, the Lord just might have someone down at the seminary waiting on you." She looked at me in amazement and replied, "A preacher!" I said, "Yes, a preacher." She said, "No way."

Well, I don't need to tell you that she is the pastor's wife of the First Baptist Church of Port Allen, Louisiana. Ann came full circle. After we had been in New Orleans several years, she was *looking* for a preacher! On registration day she would go over to the cafeteria, drink coffee, and visit with everyone who came in. She came home from one of those days and stated, "Momma, I wish this was a college and I could just go to school right here." She loved it. She continues to enjoy being a minister's wife.

Being a minister's wife is a very public role. It is one which requires the devotion and expertise of both husband and wife. While the church actually calls the pastor, they look for certain qualities and characteristics in his wife too. Often wives experience dissatisfaction because they are visible and more open to comparison than others.

Before you resent that fact, remember all public figures go through the same thing. My brother was employed by a large insurance company. He and his wife were invited to dinner by the general manager before he was hired. The manager later stated he had never given a man a job without first meeting and approving his wife.

Picture a white poster in your mind and put some round black circles on it. What do you see? Chances are you see the black dots. Yet you have all of this white expanse. Many pastors' wives let the small difficulties hide the love and privilege of being in that position in the Lord's work. Why is it we only see the problem areas—lack of money, very little time together, uncooperative deacons? We focus on all the bad things about ministry and forget the whole big white area of wonderful blessings.

The advice of one preacher's wife is to "concentrate on the pluses." Doesn't it make sense to go into ministry with a positive attitude? I hope you will accept your position as a challenge and not a duty.

Several years ago I spoke at a conference for the Fellowship of Christian Athletes in Black Mountain, North Carolina. I talked to the women and my husband talked to the men. If I had not known where I was that day, I would have thought I was in a ministers' wives class. They had the same complaints. Coaches' wives don't have any money either! Their husbands are never at home, and so on. If we are looking for the negatives, that is what we are going to find. If we can concentrate on what I like to call "the fringe benefits" of ministry, we are going to be far better off.

Let's think of some of the benefits. The first is that we are married to godly men—not perfect, but godly. Our husbands have surrendered to the ministry, trying to follow the Lord as best they can. That is a plus. Landrum always told deacons' wives who fussed about their husbands being at the church all the time, "Thank the good Lord you are a church widow, and not a beer widow!" Have you paused in gratitude for that blessing? There are a lot of unhappy women married to men who never get home with their paychecks as a result of alcohol, gambling, and sex. We hear many stories of unfaithfulness today. I am grateful to be married to a one-woman man who takes his marriage vows seriously.

I don't think we are grateful enough we are married to godly men. Tell your husband you love him and how glad you are you married him. Tell him before someone else does.

Another plus is the benefit to your children. They are going to be raised in the best environment possible. I am aware that churches are not perfect, and that church kids are not perfect, but it's a wholesome environment. Your children will meet some of the most interesting people in the world who will be wonderful role models for them.

Preachers' children meet exciting people and develop a poise other kids will miss. They are exposed at an early age to public life and its expectations. They become at home with an audience. I liken it to the poise military kids develop. We have noticed through the years of our ministry that military offspring have a lot more poise than other kids who have never moved around. They have been thrown in situations which caused them to mature quickly. Ministry is like that, and children raised in this atmosphere are truly blessed.

Many of the negative things like moving around often can be turned into pluses because of the other fringe benefits involved. A study was done of those listed in *Who's Who*, which concluded that ministers' sons were the largest category of any professional group. That's a pretty good record, I'd say.

I thank the Lord for those people who have influenced my children in a positive way. Many a Sunday School teacher went way beyond the call of duty. In fact, my son David is grown now, but Ann Massey, a friend of mine who taught him in Sunday School when he was three, *still* calls him frequently on his birthday. My daughter, Ann, had a wonderful teacher when she was in the second grade. That teacher continues to keep up with her *and* her children. Every time Ann goes back to where she grew up, she visits Mrs. Uriniak.

I'll never forget the six quail eggs Roland's teacher brought to our home to hatch. Bill Witherington brought the eggs, the cage, and all the instructions for that little project. You can imagine what a thrill it was for a small boy to have that sort of interest shown in him outside the Sunday School classroom. It was a learning experience for me also!

Jimmie Foster continues to keep up with Lan's ministry because of their teacher-pupil relationship in high school. Friends like that are pluses. Don't ever discount the nurturing support from those in your congregation, that special attention from adults.

Yes, we ministers' wives are blessed. Be positive and recall the good times and pleasant experiences. Encourage your children to remember the parsonage fun. There may be little money, but blessings galore.

I continue to be inspired by the story of a couple listening to a high-powered speaker describe his success and wealth. The wife, trying to console her husband, said, "That's OK, honey, someday you may be wealthy." His response was, "I'm wealthy now, but one day I may have money!"

If you are doing the Lord's work, you are wealthy in friends. One of the greatest pluses of this work is the support you receive from associates in churches and from other ministers and their wives.

I always get asked about the wisdom of having close friends in the congregation. Many will tell you to be wary of developing intimate friendships. These people feel it sparks jealousy and division among the members, but I don't. I would have never made it as a "loner." I *need* people—friends and relationships. Landrum and I are *not* private people. We have always had an open door and thrived on fellowship. We would not even have minded living in a pastorium next door to the church. Some of you may now be thinking we are really weird!

It occurs to me that Jesus Himself had twelve close associates. He also chose three from this group as the "inner circle" who prayed with Him and loved Him. It is a rare individual, indeed, who has no need for this kind of support.

Take it slow. It may take some time to find those individuals who can be trusted and with whom you can be open. Even then you will be disappointed on occasion. *He* was, but true friends are worth the risk.

My very best friend in the whole world lives in Gulfport, Mississippi, where we served early in our ministry. My daughter says, "Momma, I hope one day I have a friend like you do in Era." I hope she does, too. Ask God to give you those "special" people or else you invite loneliness and discontent.

As in everything, ministers' wives must use good judgment in the area of friendships. My practice has been to be warm and friendly to *everyone* at church, but if I want to invite one friend to go shopping, I do it. You may have to take the initiative on occasion because many in your congregation will probably feel you are untouchable and will be intimidated by your position. You can quickly destroy this myth by your openness and warmth.

Reuben Thomas, one of our trustees who recently passed away, had been a friend of ours for years. He went through a terrific illness. If anybody had told me he would ever walk away from that hospital bed, I would have said, "No way." But Reuben returned once to campus, giving testimony about the support he received from his Metairie Baptist Church. He talked about the thirty or more people who were willing to stay up at night, sit with him, and man the hospital room when he was so deathly ill. It really helped him recover for a time. There is no support system in the world like the people in your church. Be grateful for the blessing of friends. They really can be invaluable.

Seminary students often put off uniting with a church while they wait for that perfect opportunity. Don't do it! You will be far more attractive to a pulpit committee if you are actively serving the Lord. Use your gifts, and develop those friendships so necessary for the abundant life.

We are assisted in numerous ways. I get irritated with those ministers' wives who have pity parties about all they don't have, and about how poor they are. You are *not* poor. There are people out there in every church with incredible kindness. They do unbelievable things for their ministers, so pay attention to this outpouring of love. That is the third blessing of ministry.

Instant recognition and acceptance in a new town is the fourth benefit for a minister's family. If you move to a new city with an oil company, they don't care whether you adapt or not. However, when you move as a pastor's wife, and as a pastor, no matter what size town it is they are eager to make you feel at home. They want to introduce you and your children around. What a bonus for the clergy family to have this special place in the lives of people.

My mother-in-law always related how people reacted to her when they found out she was a preacher's wife. They would say, "Oh, you poor thing. You don't have a home because you move around." She would look at them and say, "I have lots of homes. You just have one." She felt fortunate to go to different places and be welcome at each one.

Another plus is that the church is a channel for your talents and abilities. You are a co-laborer and have the privilege of shaping lives. Someone said, "There is no greater privilege than to serve people and to watch them mature in Christlikeness." That is so true. The greatest privilege you and I have is to touch the lives of others. If I get to the end of my life and someone can say, "She was an encouragement to me," then I will feel my life has been successful.

We have the privilege of working in and through the local church with the talents and gifts God has given to us. Nowhere else will you find as many people who will help you discover and use your spiritual gifts as in the local church.

I often look back on my first experiences when I was a new pastor's wife in Charleston, Mississippi. I had never taught a Sunday School class. I didn't know *anything*. I think of the sweet, sweet people who were so patient with me. There was one particular lady, Mrs. Rice, who was seventy-two years old at that time. She was our W.M.U. president. In spite of our age difference, we had a great relationship. She called us frequently to eat a meal in her home. Those meals were especially memorable since I didn't know how to cook. I never will forget her.

At one time Landrum was distraught, to say the least. He was so mad at one of his deacons he could have shot him. This deacon had been on a deer hunt, and word came back to us that the deacon had gotten drunk and belligerent. Landrum went by Mrs. Rice's home and said, "Miss Vira" (as everybody called her), "it makes me want to lay my Bible down and go after this deacon."

She may have been the one who kept Landrum in the ministry! She looked at him and treated him just as he was acting—like a two-year-old. She told him, "Landrum, you *know* you can't lay your Bible down." She talked him out of his anger, and told him not to do anything foolish, there were better ways to handle the matter. Landrum did confront the deacon, but didn't hit him. The deacon burst into tears, apologized, and made an apology to the deacon body. The lesson here is, Miss Vira helped Landrum focus on his gift, which was ministry. People in your church will continually teach you the joy of service.

By virtue of our calling, we have unusual opportunities for influence, a built-in leadership position. Wives play a very important role in their husbands' ministry. It is like a "mom and pop" business. We are in this together and we help our husbands succeed. There is a certain innate "respect for the cloth" which causes many to look to us for counsel and leadership. You are in a key position in the church, and it has been demonstrated that wives of men in ministry have a wider sphere of influence than that of the average woman. What a plus!

Believe it or not, there are financial blessings in being a minister's wife. On occasion you will be given discounts, but don't *ever* request one. It is all right to ask for gifts to your church, but don't ask for personal favors.

If discounts do come to you, be grateful. Doctors and dentists sometimes will give you discounts or free service. Since this is not universally true, don't expect it. You may have friends who will work on your car or your home without cost or who will give you a discount on the materials you need. Many churches I know pay the pastor's utility bill. Generous individuals sometimes give you gifts for anniversaries or birthdays.

I remember the first time we went to Europe. One sweet lady came up to me and gave me fifty dollars to buy something personal while on my trip. I tell you, that was *big* money at the time! This didn't happen all the time, but occasionally, enough for me to be grateful.

Landrum and I continue to see God's blessings in the lives of our children. Ann has a diabetic condition which surfaces when she becomes pregnant, but her fourth pregnancy was the first time insulin was required. The day she learned of this problem, she came home from the doctor with a heavy heart and a one-time doctor bill of $345. The same afternoon, generous deacons brought their pastor a check for $365 to help in this crisis. Was this an accident? No—just another of God's provisions for his needy children.

So many people have fed us and entertained us. Some people have taken us on their boats and taught us and our children to ski. Activities like this were far beyond our own budget, so we appreciated them.

We belonged to a country club, although normally we could not have afforded it. They gave us a clergy membership which didn't require purchase of stock or payment of any big deposits. We simply paid small monthly dues.

When we came to New Orleans, we wanted to join the club so we could entertain groups as necessary. We discovered it had ten clergy memberships but they were filled. We added our name to the list, and expected a long wait.

However, a deacon in our church, who was a member of that club, knew we were waiting. He happened to be on one of its membership committees. He went to their meeting and said, "I want to tell you Dr. Leavell is a nice fellow. If the archbishop was on the waiting list, he would be included. Dr. Leavell is our Baptist 'archbishop,' and I think we need him in our club."

They were ashamed to add just one more clergy membership to make it eleven. That would have been too obvious. They voted to increase the number to twelve and we were included. Every time we see that deacon, he will say, "How are you doing, 'archbishop'?"

That opening came not because of who we are, but because of the position we occupy. Before you get a big head about what people do for you in the local church, let me tell you they are not doing it so much for you as for the cause you represent. Don't ever forget that. God's people choose to express love for the Lord by gifts to the pastor. That is just another reason we need to be appreciative and be good stewards of these things that come to us.

I expect many of you have already had a generous deacon figure your income tax for you. Such services are fringe benefits. You cannot buy the sort of help you get in the local church. We are helped in so many wonderful, wonderful ways. Thank the people and the Lord.

Another blessing in the ministry is travel. Travel will often come as a result of your husband's position. Our trip to the Soviet Union, for the one thousandth anniversary of the coming of Christianity to Russia, would never have happened had Landrum not been president of New Orleans Seminary. That was a fringe benefit for us. Russian Baptists invited us and three other couples to come and preach in their churches as their guests. At some point, they will come here and we will entertain them. It was a wonderful experience, but again, it was because of the position we occupy.

A Southern Baptist pastor or staff member will go to Southern Baptist Conventions on expense-paid trips by the church. You will attend state conventions. Nothing broadens you like travel, giving you a vision of missions. It is one of the great benefits of ministry, and one that will build your self-assurance. This and the many other blessings I've listed are the pluses of ministry. You can look forward to these.

There are those in every church who pray for their pastor daily. My response to these people is, "Don't miss a day." I don't want those saints to forget a single day, do you? I'm sure all of us feel that way. I want them to pray for my children and all my loved ones. I know a wonderful deacon who prays on a certain day of the week for every staff member in his church *and* their wives, by name. May his tribe increase. I want to be on every prayer list possible.

When we left Wichita Falls, Bill Pinson was interim pastor and they later called him as pastor. I remember hearing from church members about this. The question we frequently heard was, "Do you think he will make it as pastor of this church?" I never will forget Landrum's stock answer. He said, "Of course he is going to make it. Those people won't let you fail!" I hope you will be privileged someday to be in a church where the people would not let you fail. I also hope you will be worthy of that sort of love and support.

We had an International Friends program in our church. It was designed to teach English one on one to foreign wives of men stationed at our local Air Force base. I remember well the lady from Fort Worth, Texas, who led our training session. One incident has impacted my life since that time. She looked at those of us gathered in that room with an earnestness I had not felt before or since, and commanded, "Don't you dare die!" You could have heard a pin drop. Then she repeated, "Don't you dare die—until it has mattered that you lived!"

I've spent many hours thinking about that statement. I believe my life and yours have a purpose on this earth. God has blessed us in many ways. Now, what is our response?

Ask yourself this sobering question:
"Has it mattered that I lived?"
The choice is yours.
Don't miss the blessing.

APPENDIX A*

PARTNERSHIP BIBLE STUDY

After a person receives the Lord Jesus Christ, he will discover that his old nature will remain actively hungry for the things of the world .... The old nature will resist the discipline of prayer and Bible study .... Every believer... is to starve the old nature until it becomes weak and ineffective .... There is no substitute for growth, and there is no growth if there is no Bible study.

One method of Bible study which has been received enthusiastically and has proven successful...is called "partnership" Bible study .... Here is how it works.

Step 1. Choose a partner or partners. Your partner could be some other member of your family or even your entire family. If you are a young person, the one you are dating would make a logical partner, or you could choose another girl or boy or an entire group. Couples separated by military service or college find this program gives extra dimension to their correspondence. With this system of Bible study, the students are not handicapped by distance from one another.

A Christian could choose a non-Christian for a partner. This could prove to be an excellent system for sharing one's faith.

Step 2. Choose a book of the Bible for study. We suggest one of the Pauline epistles. Romans, Ephesians, and Colossians lend themselves well to the program.

Step 3. Read the first chapter of the book once a day for a week by yourself. Your partner should do the same. The chapter is not to be read in the presence of your partner, but you should be using the same translation of the Bible.

The following week, you would read the second chapter, then the third, and so on.

Step 4. Seven basics for study should be kept in mind as the chapter is read each day.
1. What is the theme of the chapter?
2. What is the key verse of the chapter?
3. What verse would you choose for memorization from the chapter?
4. What things do you learn about God the Father from the chapter?
5. What things do you learn about the Lord Jesus Christ from the chapter?
6. What things do you learn about the Holy Spirit from the chapter?
7. What things can you apply to your daily life from the chapter?
    (a) Things to do
    (b) Things to avoid

Step 5. After a week of reading the same chapter each day, fill in the answers to the above questions in your notebook. Keep the answers brief and to the point.

Step 6. On the seventh day, mail your answers to your corresponding partner, or meet with your partner or partners, and compare your results. Even the telephone can be used for this weekly contact.

Step 7. You will be surprised at how often your partner and you will disagree. The disagreement should make no difference to your work. This is one of the unique features of the program. It permits the Holy Spirit to be your Teacher. You will discover that the Holy Spirit will reveal things to you from the chapter that others will not notice. In turn, your partner(s) will discover things, by the leading of the Holy Spirit, that did not occur to you. Under no circumstances should you change your own conclusions, but you should jot down your partner's ideas on the back of your study sheet.

Step 8. Bathe the program in prayer.

There are a number of aspects of the program which fill it with vitality and life. Here are some of them.
1. The Bible is read every day.
2. Each chapter is read seven times; thus the student becomes familiar with the contents by repetition.
3. It is a personal program, enabling the Holy Spirit to be your Teacher.
4. While it is personal, it also enables you to share your spiritual discoveries with others.
5. It demands a certain discipline, for you are aware that your partner is depending on you to do your homework. You, in turn, are a challenge to your partner to be consistent.
6. You are developing a personal commentary on each book of the Bible. There is nothing so delightful as something learned directly from the Holy Spirit as He teaches you the truth from the Word of God.

7. The nature of the questions on the work sheet are designed to better acquaint you with the Lord.
8. The emphasis on personal application will have a consistent effect on your spiritual growth.
9. When this program is worked with a non-Christian it is an excellent means for sharing your faith, with the possibility of leading that one to Christ.

Appendix A is from The War Within You *(original title* Adjust or Self Destruct*), pp. 109, 111, 113-17. By Craig Massey. Copyright 1977. Moody Bible Institute of Chicago. Moody Press. Used by permission.*

APPENDIX B

WHAT IT MEANS TO BE A CHRISTIAN, OR HOW TO BE BORN AGAIN

The Bible says ...

1. "For God so loved the world, that He gave His only begotten Son, that whosoever believeth in Him should not perish, but have everlasting life" (John 3:16).
God loves us and has a purpose for our lives. There is a reason for our existence.

2. "For all have sinned, and come short of the glory of God" (Romans 3:23).
Everyone is a sinner—no exceptions. Even one act of sin separates us from God, and keeps us from fulfilling God's purpose in our lives.

3. "For the wages of sin is death; but the gift of God is eternal life through Jesus Christ our Lord" (Romans 6:23).
We (you) deserve eternal death and hell, but God loved us so much He gave His Son Jesus Christ to die for our sins.

4. "Repent therefore ... that your sins may be wiped away" (Acts 3:19).
Admit you are a sinner and in an act of will turn from your sin. You must turn to God and away from your sin.

5. "But as many as received Him, to them gave He power to become the sons of God, even to them that believe on His name" (John 1:12).

Saving faith is belief in Jesus Christ and putting your trust in Him.

6. "If thou shalt confess with thy mouth the Lord Jesus, and shalt believe in thine heart that God hath raised Him from the dead, thou shalt be saved" (Romans 10:9)

Invite Jesus into your heart and life and give Him control. This is the beginning of a wonderful new life.

7. "For whosoever shall call upon the name of the Lord shall be saved" (Romans 10:13).

This is God's promise.

Pray this prayer:

>Dear God, I know I am a sinner and I ask Your forgiveness. I want You to control my life and save me. Thank You for loving me and giving me eternal life. In Jesus' Name, Amen.

8. "As you therefore have received Christ Jesus the Lord, so walk in Him" (Colossians 2:6).

Attend a Bible-preaching church of your choice. Be baptized and become a faithful member. Worship and serve with other Christians. Read the Bible and pray each day.